# Soup & Bread

## COOKBOOK

# COOKBOOK

## Building Community
## One Pot at a Time

MARTHA BAYNE

DESIGN BY SHEILA SACHS | ILLUSTRATIONS BY PAUL DOLAN

ISBN: 978-1-950843-18-3

Parafine Press
3143 W. 33rd St. #6
Cleveland, OH 44109

Art direction and design by Sheila Sachs

*For everyone who's ever hauled a pot of soup or a bag of bread,
or just come out to eat with us on a cold winter night.*

*Thank you!*

# TABLE OF CONTENTS

# PREFACE TO THE 2020 REISSUE

SOUP & BREAD is, at its core, a tool to combat social distancing—we are all about bringing people together and fostering connection around a shared table. So it was with a heart heavy with disbelief that I had to announce in March 2020 the premature end of the year's Soup & Bread season. Two days later the Hideout, the beloved bar and music venue where friends and I have hosted Soup & Bread community meals every winter for twelve years, would be one of the many establishments closing its doors indefinitely to slow the spread of Covid-19.

As I write this in May, there's much that's unknown right now about the future of third spaces like the Hideout, about the economic precarity of our friends and neighbors, and about, frankly, the future of the food supply. We don't know when Soup & Bread will return, or what form it might take when it does. But what I do know is that the spirit fed and fostered by these weekly winter meals—and by the honest, tasty recipes in this book—endures.

When we started Soup & Bread in early 2009, at the height of that decade's economic crisis, record numbers of Chicagoans were out of work; many were losing their homes and going hungry. Friends and colleagues in my particular field, journalism, had been hit hard by the simultaneous collapse of that industry's economic model. At times it just seemed like everyone in town could use some help, or at the very least a nice bowl of soup.

Since then—and since we first published this cookbook in 2011—we have raised almost $100,000 for hunger relief efforts in Chicago, giving cash grants to a dozen neighborhood food pantries and grassroots food justice organizations each year. Sister events have been birthed around the country, in cities like Cleveland, Ohio, and in small towns like Ottawa, Illinois. Andrea Deibler, whose recipe for *khao tom* is on page 10, now runs a Soup & Bread project in Traverse City, Michigan. Former regular Dani D'Antonio moved to Lexington, Kentucky, and started a Soup & Bread there. A visiting Norwegian musician came to Soup & Bread one night and took the idea home to replicate, to wild success, at a club in Oslo.

Similarly, in the years since the *Soup & Bread Cookbook* was first published, community soup events have proliferated. In addition to the models discussed in the essays that frame each chapter of this book, there's been a boom in soup swaps and community meal projects. If I was writing this book today I would include a chapter on Queer Soup Night, an initiative born in Brooklyn and now nationwide, that uses soup as a means of raising visibility and money for LGBTQ causes. I'd write about the *comedores sociales* that sprang up in Puerto Rico in the aftermath of Hurricane Maria, serving free soup and more to all comers. And I'd write, for sure, about the countless soup-based relief efforts that have been launched since the pandemic threw 22 million Americans (and counting) out of work.

Here in Chicago, food pantries are seeing ever-longer lines even as their volunteer bases are dwindling. Wrigley Field and the United Center, homes to the Cubs and the Bulls, have been turned into food distribution hubs. The national nonprofit Feeding America estimates that nationwide an additional 17 million people will seek supplemental food assistance in the coming months. Our work is a drop in this swelling ocean of need, but since Soup & Bread ceased programming in March our community has come together in new and creative ways. We've supported the efforts of one pantry in our network to distribute bags of produce to suddenly unemployed hospitality workers, and helped get groceries to a Hideout bartender who launched a free meal service for those in need. We've volunteered at pantries ourselves and helped deliver groceries to the elderly. One of us works as a grocer; another is busy sewing homemade masks. Across the city our community has mobilized to generate the mutual aid to which Soup & Bread is in service.

We made the decision to bring back our out-of-print cookbook in that same spirit. Half the royalties from sales of this book will be donated to the Greater Chicago Food Depository, the food bank serving Chicago food pantries. The other half will be donated to grassroots hunger-relief and mutual aid organizations.

As I was pulling together material for this reprint, I spent some time looking back through photos of the past decade-plus of Soup & Bread events. There are a lot of photos of soup—so many bowls of soup—but also many of friends and strangers, and of strangers who became friends, gathered in joyous, gentle chaos in the back room of the Hideout to eat and drink together. I marvel still at the miracle of it all. We are so lucky to have each other.

Some of the restaurants featured in the pages that follow have closed, and some soup cooks have moved on to other places and pastimes; in that sense, this reprint is a snapshot of a moment gone by. But I remain confident that the collective moments of fellowship and care these cooks and hundreds more helped create will come roaring back in the years to come. In the meantime, I trust that you who are reading this are all safe and sound and housed, and that you are able to share meals with people you love. This book can help.

Martha Bayne
May 2020

On a raw evening in Chicago, in the middle of March, the back room of one little bar is a happy mess of connections—social networking embodied, no wifi required.

In that room, in the glow of strings of twinkly lights and under the silent gaze of several stuffed and mounted fish, you'd find a gardener, a mom, and an actor, a writer and a farmer, a country singer, a social worker, and 75 others eating, talking, and standing in line. A harried bartender is spilling drinks and crumbs are flying as a graphic designer runs a knife through a baguette. A Michelin-starred chef shares cooking tips with a vegan barista. A DJ spins deep cuts of obscure R&B and at least two kids—maybe more, hard to tell—are running around in a ginger-ale-fueled frenzy.

The gardener runs the program at the school where the kids grow peppers. She's working on a new project with the writer, who's chatting up an editor, and introducing her to the kids' mom, who brought her friend the musician. He's an avid home baker, a loaf of fresh sourdough under his arm, and the actor tries to distract him long enough to snag a bite. Across the room, the social worker—who's friends with the gardener—is chatting with the DJ, whom she knows from back in the day, but she's interrupted by the chef, who is wondering if the DJ does parties.

Faded cotton tablecloths and candles in colored globes dress up tables of varying sizes, and over on a small rolling bar, dollar bills—ones, fives, the occasional twenty—pile up in a busted Crock-Pot, vintage 1974. At the rear of the room a hand-painted wooden sign hangs above an empty stage. For now the action is in front of the stage, where two long tables provide the catalyst for all this good cheer.

Behind the tables stand half a dozen apron-clad cooks, wielding ladles and fielding questions. Before them diners file past, clutching paper bowls and jockeying for space.

What's on the table? On the table is soup.

Soup is an all-purpose dish. It's nutritious, inexpensive, and infinitely variable. It can be an earthy meal in a chipped pottery bowl or an elegant palate cleanser, frothed into a porcelain cup. It can showcase the explosive flavor of fresh spring peas and provide refuge for tired celery and stale bread. It soothes the sick, it nourishes the poor—and it can trick children into eating their veggies. But perhaps more than any other food, soup can also be a powerful tool: drawing people together and helping them reach out to others.

You're probably familiar with the "stone soup" fable—the tale of hungry townspeople who feed themselves when each contributes a measly carrot or potato to the pot. I think I first heard it in preschool, when it served as the foundation of a lesson in cooperation and sharing. As an adult I've come across it in multiple cookbooks, where the moral of the story skews more toward the way cooking can create dishes that are greater than the sum of their parts. The true power of soup, I believe, falls somewhere in the middle—in its ability to serve as both potent metaphor and cheap, tasty dinner.

I began to learn this firsthand a few years ago, after I had left my job as an alt-weekly editor on the food beat, moved to Wisconsin, and tried to write a book. That didn't work out so well, and by the winter of 2009 I was back in Chicago and tending bar at the Hideout, a ramshackle, Depression-era tavern on a dusty industrial street.

The Hideout is one of the city's coziest and most eclectic music clubs, showcasing everything from country to experimental jazz on the little stage in the back. But early Wednesday evenings, when I was on duty, there wasn't anything to do but polish the pint glasses. Garbage trucks and snowplows lumbered down Wabansia Street round the clock, en route to a city garage, but what little happy-hour business I saw came mainly from shoppers at the nearby Home Depot. But that winter the recession hit the city hard, and even thirsty home remodelers were scarce. It was cold. I was lonely. And then one night it occurred to me to serve soup.

I asked around and some friends said sure—they'd come out on Wednesdays if there was food. So I thrifted a bunch of mismatched bowls and started a blog and a Facebook page to get the word out. I knew a lot of cooks, professional and not, and

I hit them up to contribute. "Bring a couple gallons of soup some Wednesday," I said. "Any kind of soup at all. We'll have day-old bread and hot soup and it'll be fun, and we'll take a collection for a good cause. It's called, 'Soup & Bread.'"

On the first night I wasn't sure what to expect. It was the Wednesday after New Year's, it was snowing, and a gas main had broken at the corner. A friend had surprised me with a load of secondhand slow cookers at Christmas, and when I showed up to plug them in the entire block was lousy with fire engines and hazmat trucks. But despite this confusing scene a handful of determined diners navigated the roadblock and found their way to the bar. They shook off the snow and perched on stools to slurp soups donated by one of the other bartenders, by a friend's pastry chef sister, and by a nearby café. The food was free, but we put out a bucket for donations, and we collected more than $100 for the Greater Chicago Food Depository.

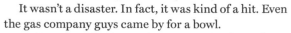

It wasn't a disaster. In fact, it was kind of a hit. Even the gas company guys came by for a bowl.

Since then, for three winters running, the Hideout has hosted a weekly Soup & Bread feast, courtesy of professional and amateur cooks—musicians and artists, restaurateurs and farmers, writers, parents, food geeks, and friends—all of whom donate homemade soup to serve along with donated bread to crowds of 100 or more. Diners are free to contribute a dollar or 20—whatever they can afford—and the take is passed along to local food pantries, a different one each week. It's an easy, low-key way to get people out of the house and socializing in the dead of darkest winter, and as word has spread we've raised more than $13,000 (so far) for a critical cause. According to a recent report from the nonprofit Feeding America, an estimated 37 million people nationwide now rely on food from food banks, pantries, and soup kitchens—a 46 percent increase in over just four years.

When people ask, I usually describe Soup & Bread as an "everybody wins" type of project. Diners get food, cooks get glory, the bar gets business, and the food pantries get funds. "Soup & Bread is permaculture," Los Angeles–based writer and "urban homesteader" Erik Knutzen told me once. Because what is permaculture other than the creation of a self-sustaining, mutually beneficial system?

At Soup & Bread we're not going to school you in the virtues of local, seasonal cooking, but there are many farmers and sustainable food advocates in the mix. We're not out to celebrate celebrity, but some of Chicago's hottest chefs have hopped on board. It speaks in its own way to the joys of off-the-grid eating, expressed by everything from underground dinners and food trucks to charitable DIY events like Brooklyn's annual "Pie in the Park" fundraiser. It's a gentle way of raising popular awareness about poverty, hunger, and nutrition. And, of course, it's fun.

It was so much fun, in fact, that along with my friend Sheila Sachs I took it on the road to Brooklyn in 2010. That hazy, joyous night at the Bell House raised $900 and had me scrubbing Crock-Pots over a slop sink surrounded by strippers wearing not much besides tattoos and sequined pasties. We hit the road again a year later, journeying to Seattle to the Funhouse, a great little punk bar in the shadow of the Space Needle.

At the end of Soup & Bread's first year I asked Sheila—the graphic designer with the bread knife—to help me compile recipes from Soup & Bread cooks into a cookbook. We were inspired by the community cookbooks our moms had had when we were kids—those mimeographed fundraisers for the parish or middle school loaded with recipes for crab dip and green bean casserole—only our community was, you know, a bar.

The book was spiral-bound with a letterpress cover and illustrations by our friend Paul Dolan. It was also, if I may say so, super cute. For a year or so we set up shop at craft fairs all over Chicago and sold copies on consignment around town. Out of town, we enlisted our moms as regional sales reps.

As we got out in the world and talked to people about Soup & Bread, people started seeking us out to talk soup. We heard stories about regional soup traditions, about soup swaps and salons and family soup Sundays. My friend Ben told me about a soup circle he and his friends started and kept alive for several years. And my college housemate reminded me, to my amnesiac amazement, that for a while senior year we tried to instigate a Friday soup dinner as an alternative to the pizza and beer that dominated campus weekends.

Soup, in short, is everywhere.

Why does something so simple resonate with so many people? I think in part because it sits so snugly at the intersection of a lot of cultural trends. Map a Venn diagram of the recession, the boom in home cooking, and increased awareness of the lifelong benefits of good nutrition, and in the middle you'll find a bowl of soup.

That's where this book comes in—a revised and expanded edition of the first self-published cookbook of recipes from Soup & Bread nights paired with stories about soup and other soup projects.

As a writer I've always been more interested in the stories behind the stuff on your plate than in mastering new levels of adjectival gymnastics to describe the taste of tuna. So as a writer-turned-soup-wrangler, I set out to talk to people about their soup stories, and to collect evidence that now, perhaps more than ever, soup is bringing people together to serve a common good.

The concept's been around forever—or since the Middle Ages, at least—when European monasteries offered free soup and bread to hungry petitioners at the gate. More recently, of course, the soup line is a defining image of the Great Depression, when soup kitchens nationwide provided hot meals to millions of struggling Americans. But not every soup project is steeped in history. Here in Chicago, the power of soup has been harnessed to fund grants for artists and to spread the gospel of local, sustainable, seasonal eating.

Soup can be a political statement: the radical volunteers of Food Not Bombs (the subject of Chapter Seven) have been providing free vegetarian soup to the hungry as a protest against war and social injustice since 1980.

Or it can be performance art: In 2003 Bill Drummond, who once burned £1 million cash as front man for the band The KLF, launched an erratic performance piece called the "Soup Line," in which he traveled to the homes of complete strangers across Britain and Ireland and cooked them a pot of soup. (There's more about that in Chapter Five.)

Soup can be a way to strengthen social ties. According to sociologist Juliet Schor, soup swaps (Chapter Two) are a micro-manifestation of how the recession has inspired communities to come together. "Soup may seem like a small thing," she told National Public Radio in 2010. "But it may turn out that your sharing network is very important to you if you lose your job, if your housing is in jeopardy. You're going to have these folks to rely on."

Soup can be a way of fostering a connection to home and family (Chapter One), or just a means of honing your culinary skills to feed your friends (Chapter Eight).

"It's simple and it's mutually comprehensible to anyone," one of the members of InCUBATE, a Chicago arts collective, told me, talking about their Sunday Soup fundraising project (also Chapter Five). "The nice thing is there's a simple core that people can layer their own concerns, issues, ways of working on top of. And just because the thing at the middle is simple, it doesn't mean everything else can't be more complicated or contextually specific."

I don't think he realized at the time that he could have been talking about soup itself.

All these soup-based efforts have in common the desire to extend hospitality to all comers. To forge community in the moment, over the table, or across years. And they are, I've come to see, as forgiving and flexible as soup itself. They feed crowds, raise money, stimulate creativity, and—like the Campbell's ad says, help you "get to a happier place."

Lisa Lee is the executive director of the Jane Addams Hull-House Museum, whose Re-Thinking Soup project is the subject of Chapter Six. In our wide-ranging conversation about community, history, and social justice, and about the responsibility of cultural institutions to "foster radical democracy," we talked about the strange power of soup to stir all these ideas into one easy-to-digest pot.

"It's not easy to have a soup kitchen in a bar," she said. "Like, really? It is hard. But it's also super joyful, right?"

She's right. It is. And it beats polishing pint glasses.

*There's a whole lot more about Soup & Bread on our website at soupandbread.net.*

## ABOUT THE RECIPES IN THIS BOOK

SOUP & BREAD depends on the creative energies of forever growing crew of volunteer cooks, and so does this book. Every recipe found within (with the exception of one, just to prove the rule) was prepared for and served at a Soup & Bread dinner in Chicago, Brooklyn, or Seattle. Taken as a whole it's a document of what we ate, with whom—a true community cookbook that reflects the way people talk about cooking and eating.

Of course, it's intended to be a useful guide to cooking as well. To that end I've tried to present directions as clearly as possible, pestering contributors to pin down the size of that "can of beans," and find out just how long "cook all day" means. I hope I've preserved the cooks' idiosyncratic voices. Any errors or misjudgments made in that effort are my own.

Structurally, this book is a little loose compared to traditional cooking primers. Recipes are organized not by ingredients, but by associations—and pork, chicken, squash, and split peas may often wantonly rub up against each other in the same chapter, or the same recipe. To make things easy, all the recipes are listed in the back by type: poultry, seafood, the various meats, and vegan and vegetarian-friendly soups. For the latter, you may need to just trade the chicken stock for vegetable.

And, it's true: While the title of the book promises soup and bread, bread is comparatively underrepresented. To help you find the bread recipes awash in all this soup, they've been indexed as well, and are italicized in the table of contents.

Most of the recipes are pretty simple, but even the fancier ones are accessible to an ambitious home cook, and few require any special gear beyond a large stockpot and a ladle. But a couple of handy gadgets do pop up here and there—most notably blenders. Throughout, if a recipe directs you to "blend" or "puree" you've got two options: Carefully decant your soup into a stand blender, in batches, or use a hand-held immersion blender (a "stick blender") to puree in the pot.

Other useful tools include cheesecloth and a chinois, the fine-mesh conical sieve that's a staple of restaurant kitchens and a boon if you want to smooth a pureed soup to a velvety polish; and a mandoline, which can make slicing veggies a breeze.

Finally, though every effort has been made to ensure that recipes are original to their creators, recipes are not subject to copyright protection (though the language used to describe them is). Per the guidelines of the International Association of Culinary Professionals, we've given credit for creative adaptations as due. Beyond that I can only hope that any established cook who stumbles upon a vaguely familiar recipe in this book will appreciate the homage.

# CHAPTER ONE

# Soup from Home

*In* the down-at-heel dining room of a former convent on Chicago's far north side, dinner was served. Senegalese Afropop blasted from the CD player, and an ebullient toddler bounced underfoot as a dozen men, women, and teenage girls hustled in and out of the kitchen, setting the table with limeade and salad and a huge pan of chilaquiles.

The convent is home to the Heartland Alliance's Marjorie Kovler Center, a human-rights organization providing support to survivors of torture as they build new lives in Chicago. Every other Friday the center hosts what's known, without fuss, as "cooking night"—at which a different cook prepares a meal from his or her homeland. In attendance this particular night were diners from Togo and Haiti, Eritrea and Pakistan—and between the music and the teenagers and the polyglot of language it was hard to get a word in edgewise. But when I mentioned that I was working on a cookbook about the ways people conjure community through soup— people around the world, I added, with the bravado of the generalist—one woman, a volunteer, piped up.

"There's no soup in Côte d'Ivoire."

What did I know? Why would a hot West African country have any use for soup? But it turned out, I discovered later, that soup truly is universal. From pho to gazpacho to gumbo, soup is everywhere. Even in Côte d'Ivoire, where, it's true, most meals are built around cassava and plantains, a host might trot out a chilled avocado soup for a special occasion. "The truth is," says Janet Clarkson, in her compact and thoroughly enjoyable *Soup: A Global History*, "the idea of soup is not even vaguely unfamiliar to anyone, anywhere, on this entire planet."

Soup, Clarkson argues, is the foundation of civilization. Cultures worldwide learned to cook by boiling grains in water. Over time they added vegetables and, on occasion, meat. And from the porridges and potages of the early days evolved split pea soup and congee, mushroom barley and groundnut stew. Now even Antarctica can lay claim to a signature soup—a tasty "hooch" of pemmican, oatmeal, and water, seasoned perhaps with seal blubber, cherished by explorers and ceremonially eaten on Midsummer's Day.

While Antarctic explorers may not miss their hooch once they're off the ice, soup can conjure powerful associations. The Kovler Center's cooking night is a means of fostering a sense of security and community among traumatized, displaced people through the universal ritual of creating and sharing a meal. I wound up there because some of the center's clients had brought soup to Soup & Bread earlier in the year. One of them, Chantal Powell, a chic young woman with a head of luxurious braids, brought Haitian Independence Soup, a treat from her native Haiti.

Also known as "soupe giraumond" or, in Creole, "soup joumou," the rich, mildly spicy puree of pumpkin or squash and beef was, under French colonial rule, a delicacy for the rich; enslaved Africans had to stretch their soup with bread and scraps of inferior meat. Now soupe giraumond is eaten every New Year's Day across Haiti—and in Haitian communities around the world—to celebrate the day that country won its independence and became the world's first free black republic. (See page 5 for Chantal's rendition.)

In other contexts, soup can connect families to their roots. Mariana Glusman's grandmother fled the pogroms in Ukraine as a teenager and wound up with one sister in Argentina. The rest of her family was set to follow, but the Iron Curtain crashed down and it was 50 years before the sisters saw their siblings again. Though the family eventually moved from Argentina to Mexico City, where Mariana was born, to the United States, the recipe for grandma's borscht was passed along. "It's cool," says Mariana, a pediatrician in Chicago. "Soup is the one thing that remains of a culture that's lost to my family. It's a legacy of something long gone." Mariana's parents still serve borscht on special occasions, but thanks to Mariana's peripatetic background, it's not beets but chicken tortilla soup that's her go-to comfort food.

Lawyer Peter Tyksinski, raised in suburban Chicago, has similar cross-cultural soup cravings. He's lived in Tokyo for almost six years and has learned to enjoy miso soup every morning for breakfast. But on the weekends he prepares the split pea and bean soups he craves from home. "I can trace my first memories of soup to my mom's rendition of green split pea with a giant ham hock," he says. "Prying the meat out from under the tough ribbon of skin and eating it was a perverse joy. As wonderful as Japanese soups can be, there is something much more fulfilling about making my own."

My friend Irma Nuñez also lived in Japan for many years. She recalls longingly the pleasures of her favorite ramen shops, on a bustling ring road near her first Tokyo apartment. "It was so amazingly good and comforting," she says, that even after she moved across town she would regularly trek back to Nogata for ramen. Nowadays, she treks to the Asian malls in Chicago's far suburbs for a fix of the real thing. And she does so in spite of an intolerance for gluten. "I could live without pizza and cheeseburgers," she says. "But I don't think I can say the same for ramen."

Like Irma's ramen shops—whose offerings changed depending what side of the street you were on—soups around the world reflect the peculiarities of their region and their cooks. Just ask an insider about the difference between Filipino lugao and Thai khao tom (page 10) and—or any number of similar rice porridges found across Asia. Or Russian and Polish borscht (page 16). Or, heck, Manhattan and New England clam chowder (page 20).

*Following are 14 recipes for soups that can deliver a potent sense of place, whether that place is halfway around the world or just down the interstate. They're paired with a recipe for "free-range" sourdough bread, a bread technique as old as cooking itself.*

These idiosyncrasies are part of why soup can be a touchstone of home. A few years ago my friend Shana, a Jewish girl from Saint Louis, married Simo, a Muslim from Marrakech. While they were courting Simo told Shana of his mother's cooking—lavishing praise on her harrira, the lamb stew eaten during Ramadan to break the fast. When Shana went to Morocco to meet the family, harrira was the first thing her future mother-in-law cooked for her.

"It was clear after I tasted it," says Shana, "that I was going to have to learn to cook it myself."

Harrira (page 6) is traditionally eaten at sundown across Morocco during Ramadan—or after a long night of partying at a wedding. Everyone makes it differently, Simo says. "But it's always a collective event. Harrira is about generosity. You always make sure to make extra, so that there's some for people who are hungry."

When Simo and Shana's son was born, Simo's mother, LaZahra, came to Chicago to help care for the baby. Shana does the grocery shopping and LaZahra does most of the cooking, schooling her daughter-in-law in the finer points of Moroccan cusine.

Now, says Simo, "when I see my mom making harrira, I feel like family is here, and I am so happy."

# HAITIAN INDEPENDENCE SOUP
*from*
## CHANTAL POWELL

Chantal jotted down the bones of this recipe as we waited for dinner to start at the Kovler Center. The soup's traditionally made with boiled beef, but she's a vegetarian, so I've included the meat as an option only. It's very important to chop the vegetables quite small, she says, but it's the cilantro that's key to the soup's success, so don't be shy. "That," she says, "is where the whole taste is sitting."

### INGREDIENTS        SERVES 8

- **1** large butternut squash, peeled and cubed
- water
- **1** tablespoon sugar
- **1** tablespoon olive oil
- **1** yellow onion, small dice
- **2** carrots, small dice
- **3** ribs celery, small dice
- **1** turnip, peeled and diced
- **1** large potato, peeled and diced (optional)
- **2** cloves garlic, minced
- **1** bunch cilantro, roughly chopped
- **1** cube vegetable bouillon
- **1** pound cooked, shredded beef (optional)
- salt and pepper

### PREPARATION

In large pot, cover squash with water, add sugar, and bring to a boil. Let simmer until squash is quite soft, then blend into a smooth puree. Add more water if it gets too thick.

Chop vegetables very small—into ½-inch bits or so. In a large stock pot, sauté onion, carrot, and celery until soft. Then add turnip and potato (if desired), and a dash or two of salt and pepper. Sauté another few minutes, then add garlic and reduce heat. Simmer over low heat until garlic is translucent.

Pour squash puree into pot, adding water to achieve desired consistency, then add cilantro, more salt and pepper, and bouillon cube. Add beef now if desired. Bring to a rolling boil for 5 minutes, then reduce heat and "let it go." The longer it simmers, the better it tastes.

Chantal Powell is from Haiti and learned to cook from her mom, who ran a restaurant and a hospitality school. She has been in Chicago for ten years. She hopes you enjoy the joumou/giraumont soup from her country.

# HARRIRA
*from*
## SHANA PEARLMUTTER AND LAZAHRA RAJIB

Shana collaborated with her mother-in-law, LaZahra, on this rendition of the savory Moroccan staple served daily during Ramadan. "As everyone breaks the fast at the very same time, there is very little conversation," says Shana. "Families say 'Bismillah'—a blessing of thanks to Allah—and then all that is heard are a lot of slurps, while this lovely soup is eaten out of hand-carved, lemon-wood spoons all over Morocco." It's eaten with soft, chewy dates, boreks (fried, stuffed phyllo-type pastries) and a lot of fresh juices. LaZahra could make this soup in her sleep, but pinning her down on measurements was difficult, so Shana pieced together a few published recipes to approximate her take on this aromatic yet subtly seasoned soup.

**INGREDIENTS**                    SERVES 6

- **1** pound (or so) boneless lamb shoulder
- **2** tablespoons extra virgin olive oil
- **2** small brown onions, chopped
- **2** large garlic cloves, crushed
- **1½** teaspoons cumin
- **1½** teaspoons ground black pepper
  salt
- **2** teaspoons paprika
- **1** teaspoon turmeric
- **¼** teaspoon ginger
  dash of cinnamon
- **1** cup finely chopped Italian parsley
- **1** cup finely chopped cilantro
- **1** bay leaf
  generous pinch of saffron threads
- **2** tablespoons tomato paste
- **1** 29-ounce can of chopped tomatoes (LaZahra blends the tomatoes, along with their juice and the tomato paste, in the blender with about a tablespoon of flour before she adds it to the soup)
- **4** cups water (or beef or vegetable stock if you like)
- **1½** cups lentils
- **2** 15-ounce cans chickpeas (rinse and drain before use)
  handful vermicelli noodles (optional)
- **1** lemon

## PREPARATION

Place the lamb, turmeric, black pepper, garlic, salt, ginger, cinnamon, olive oil, onion, cilantro, and parsley into a large soup pot over a low heat. Stir frequently for 5 minutes. Pour pureed tomatoes into the mixture and let simmer for 15 minutes.

Pour in 4 cups water or stock, then add bay leaf and lentils to the pot. Bring to a boil, then reduce the heat to simmer and add saffron. Let simmer, covered, for 2 hours.

About 10 minutes before serving turn the heat to medium high, add chickpeas and noodles (if desired); let cook about 10 minutes, until noodles are al dente.

Serve topped with chopped cilantro and a squeeze of lemon on top.

Shana Pearlmutter is a painter, an art teacher at Bell Elementary School in Chicago, and, in her words, a collector of ephemera and random objects.

LaZahra Rajib is a mother to many on two continents, and, per Shana, one of the best Moroccan chefs ever to dice onions, split saffron, or toss couscous.

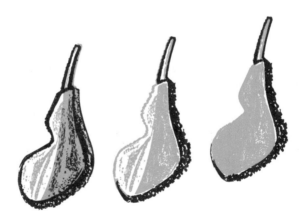

# MARAK BAMIA
## (Lamb-Okra Soup)
*from*
### KHAWLA SHUHAYIB

In 2009 we asked Scott Waguespack, the alderman for Chicago's 32nd Ward—home of the Hideout and our Soup & Bread—if he would contribute a soup, and he agreed, but he outsourced the cooking to his friend Khawla. She and her daughter Rawasi brought two traditional Iraqi soups to the party one frosty winter night. Khawla doesn't use recipes, but a friend came close to an approximation of hers by loosely adapting this one from Kay Karim's *Iraqi Family Cookbook*. According to Khawla's husband, Najim, a marak is typically thick and often made with tomatoes, closer to a stew than a soup.

## INGREDIENTS                    SERVES 12

- **3** pounds lamb neck bones
- **2** package of frozen okra, thawed, cut into 1-inch pieces
- **1** 12-ounce can tomato sauce
- **1** 6-ounce can tomato paste
- **½** a head of garlic, crushed
  vegetable oil
- **8** cups water
- **2** teaspoons salt

## PREPARATION

Boil lamb neck bones until tender. Drain, return to pot, add okra, and sauté gently in oil for a few minutes. Add tomato sauce, paste, and water and bring up heat slowly, stirring occasionally. Add garlic. Simmer 10 minutes. Serve with rice.

Khawla Shuhayib has a degree in physical education from the University of Basra in Iraq, and she currently works as a housekeeper at the Palmer House. She's lived in Chicago since June 27, 2007.

# KIMCHI CHIGAE

*from*

## MIKE SULA

Mike has contributed to Soup & Bread several years running, and each time he's brought a soup more unusual than the last. In 2011 it was an elaborately constructed Japanese oden; in 2010 he test-drove an experiment using Asian carp. But this soup, from 2009, remains my favorite of his offerings. Kimchi chigae is infinitely variable—it's sort of the Korean version of back-of-the-refrigerator soup. As Mike says, "You can add anything you like: tofu, seafood, beef, pork belly. Hot dogs and Spam became popular ingredients after GIs introduced them to Korea. The only essentials are liquid—water will do—and kimchi, preferably the old stuff, super sour and fermented until fizzy."

### INGREDIENTS                     SERVES 16

- **6** pounds pork neck bones
  stock vegetables—an onion, a head of garlic, halved on the equator, a peeled carrot, a couple of celery stalks, and a red bell pepper
- **8** cups kimchi, approximately two months old
- **1** pound bulgogi (sliced, marinated beef, like Korean Italian beef)
- **3** tablespoons gochuchang (Korean red pepper paste), or to taste
- **2** bunches green onions, cut into 2-inch pieces
- **2** packages firm tofu, pressed under plates, drained, and cut into ½-inch pieces

### PREPARATION

Roast the neck bones at 350°F for 1 hour. Cover with water in a large stockpot and simmer at the lowest possible heat for 4–8 hours. Add the stock vegetables 1 hour before finishing. Strain though cheesecloth, spoon off the fat, discard the solids.

In a separate pan, brown the bugolgi until heated through. Add it, plus the kimchi with its juice and the red pepper paste, to about a gallon and a half of stock. Bring to a boil, reduce heat, and simmer for an hour or so. Add the tofu and onions during the last 20 minutes, then cooked rice or noodles if you like.

Mike Sula is a food writer for the *Chicago Reader*.

# KHAO TOM

*from*

## ANDREA DEIBLER AND ALLISON STOUT

Khao tom is Thai comfort food—a soothing rice porridge found in various forms all over Asia. Also known as jook or congee, it's a popular breakfast dish in Cambodia and Malaysia, sickbed food in Korea and Japan, and a classic late-night snack just about everywhere. It can be a thick paste or a watery gruel; spicy with ginger and chiles or bland enough for a fussy baby. Andrea and Allison, two savvy cooks, collaborated on this version in 2009.

**INGREDIENTS**                    SERVES 8

CHICKEN

| | |
|---|---|
| 3-4 | pound roaster chicken |
| 3 | cloves garlic |
| ¼ | onion, thickly sliced |
| 1 | lime, halved (lemon or orange can be substituted) |
| 4 | slices bacon |
| | kosher salt and pepper |
| | kitchen twine |

SOUP

| | |
|---|---|
| 9 | cups chicken stock |
| 1 | bunch of scallions, sliced |
| ¼ | cup cilantro leaves, picked |
| 2 | tablespoons fish sauce |
| 3 | tablespoons rice wine vinegar, divided |
| 4 | tablespoons soy sauce |
| 1 | teaspoon chili flakes in a tea infuser (or tied up in cheesecloth) |
| 4 | cups cooked basmati or jasmine rice |
| 1 | stalk lemon grass, peeled to center, bottom only |
| | salt and pepper to taste |

GARNISH

wonton wrappers
canola or vegetable oil
kosher salt
juice of 1 lime

## PREPARATION

CHICKEN: Preheat oven to 375°F. Remove the giblets and rinse the chicken in cold water. Pat dry inside and out with paper towels. Sprinkle outside of chicken and cavity liberally with salt and pepper. Stuff cavity with garlic, onion, and lime. Tie the legs together with kitchen twine and tuck the wing tips under the body. Wrap bacon over the chicken breast and roast on a rack, breast side up, until a thermometer inserted in the thigh reads 165°F. Let the chicken rest and cool for at least a half an hour. Remove thighs and breasts from the chicken. Remove the meat from the bones, discarding the skin. Cut the cooked breast and leg meat into ½-inch squares.

WONTONS: Heat 1½ inch oil in a deep, heavy pot over moderately high heat until a thermometer registers 360°F. Slice wonton wrappers into strips about 3 inches by half an inch.

Gently lay 10 strips on oil and fry, turning over once, until golden, 15 to 30 seconds total. Transfer with a slotted spoon to paper towels to drain. Fry the remaining wonton strips 10 at a time. Sprinkle with lime juice (do not soak, wontons will become soggy) and season with salt.

THE REST: Cook the rice according to the package's instructions using chicken stock in place of water (if using water, add 1 teaspoon salt). Add 1 tablespoon rice wine vinegar when the rice is cooked. Set aside.

Heat the chicken stock slowly to 165°F. While heating, add the lemon grass and the tea infuser of chili flakes. Once the stock is hot, add fish sauce, soy sauce, and remaining vinegar, seasoning with more salt and pepper to taste. Remove lemon grass and infuser. Add the cooked chicken.

To serve, put ½ cup of the rice into each soup bowl. Ladle the hot soup on top of the rice and garnish liberally with the scallions, cilantro, and wonton crisps.

Andrea Deibler is the head butcher at City Provisions, a local, sustainable deli.

Allison Stout is in charge of savory pies at Hoosier Mama Pie Company and provides catering, cooking instruction, and personal chef services under the name Seriously Good Food.

# DORO WETT
*from*
## BRIAN FERGUSON

This recipe is based on traditional cooking instructions for doro wett, which is essentially the Ethiopian national dish. A thick, rich chicken stew usually eaten with pieces of spongy flatbread called injera, it's made with a spicy clarified butter known as niter kibbeh and a pungent mixture of North African spices called berbere. Garnished with whole boiled eggs and spiked with lime juice, this hearty midday meal can carry you through the whole day.

**INGREDIENTS**                    SERVES 12

NITER KIBBEH
- **1** pound butter
- **½** yellow onion
- **1** tablespoon minced garlic
- **2** tablespoons finely grated ginger
- **1** teaspoon turmeric
- **⅛** teaspoon ground cardamom
- **1** inch cinnamon stick
- **1** whole clove
- **⅛** teaspoon nutmeg

BERBERE
- **1** teaspoon fenugreek seeds
- **½** cup dried serrano chile (known as balin/tipico in Mexican groceries)
- **½** cup paprika
- **2** tablespoons kosher salt
- **2** teaspoons ground ginger
- **2** teaspoons onion powder
- **1** teaspoon fresh ground cardamom
- **1** teaspoon ground nutmeg
- **½** teaspoon garlic powder
- **¼** teaspoon ground cloves
- **¼** teaspoon ground cinnamon
- **¼** teaspoon ground allspice

## DORO WETT

- **1** small red onion, chopped
- **2** carrots, small dice
- **1** stalk celery, small dice
- **1** large green bell pepper, medium dice
- **⅓** cup of berbere spice mix
- **¼** cup niter kebbeh
- **3** cloves garlic, chopped
- **½** teaspoon black peppercorns
- **½** teaspoon cardamom pods
- **3** cloves
- **1** tablespoon tomato paste
- **1** small starchy potato, peeled, halved, and sliced thin
- **⅓** cup red wine
- **1** tablespoon kosher salt
- **2** tablespoons rice wine vinegar
- **2** pounds chicken, skinless, boneless thigh meat, whole pieces
- **8** cups good chicken stock
- **¼** cup lime juice
- **12** large eggs

## PREPARATION

NITER KIBBEH: Add the spices to a small saucepan and stir on low heat for a few minutes. Cut the butter into smaller pats and add in all at once. Stir until butter is melted then turn the flame down as low as possible and simmer 45 minutes, or until milk solids have sunk to the bottom of the pot. Strain carefully, preferably with micro-mesh filter. This will be more than you need, but it stores well in a cool cabinet for a couple of weeks or in the fridge for several months.

BERBERE: Mix all and grind fine.

DORO WETT: In a large pot (3 gallons or more) over medium-high heat combine the niter kebbeh, onions, carrots, celery, and half of the green peppers and sauté for 7–10 minutes until soft and starting to caramelize. Add half of the berbere and sauté another 5 minutes, frequently scraping the bottom of the pot. Add the rest of the ingredients except for the lime juice, eggs, and yellow squash. Stir well then simmer for 30 minutes. Remove the chicken, cool briefly, then chop. Return the chicken to the pot as well as the yellow squash and simmer for 15 minutes.

In a separate pot, hard-boil the eggs, cool, peel, and with a toothpick or paring knife, make small holes/incisions around each egg while keeping it whole. Add the eggs and the lime juice to soup and let marinate for 20 minutes with the heat turned off. Reheat if necessary, and serve.

Brian Ferguson is the owner of BigBite Catering in Chicago.

# POZOLE
*from*
## DAVID HAMMOND

David has made this rich and rustic take on a Mexican classic a Soup & Bread tradition, preparing it three years in a row. The first two batches featured meat from Ermine, a mulefoot pig he'd purchased as a piglet from the Rock Creek Mill and Heritage Farm in Argyle, Wisconsin. David followed—and documented—Ermine's life from farm to fork as part of an ongoing effort to become a more conscious carnivore. "Mulefoots, a heritage breed, yield excellent pork," he says. "You won't find it at the big supermarkets, so I'd recommend using any fatty piece of pork, like a shoulder chop. I used chops, a hambone, and neck bones. The better the pork, the better the pozole." By the third year Ermine was but a fond memory, but the pozole was still very tasty.

## INGREDIENTS                    SERVES 12

- **3** pounds of pork soup bones (knuckles, ribs, neck)
- **2 ½** pounds of pork shoulder
- **1** bay leaf
- **5** cloves garlic
- **2** medium onions
- **1** carrot
- **3** pounds hominy
- **4** tablespoons cal (lye)
- **9** fresh jalapenos (charred, peeled, and chopped)
- **12** chiles de arbol (crumbled)
- **2** teaspoons oregano
- **4** teaspoons cumin
- **4** tablespoons chili powder
- water
- salt to taste

## PREPARATION

Roast pork bones and meat at 350°F for about 45 minutes. Put bones and meat in a 5-gallon pot filled almost to the brim with water. Add bay leaf, 2 garlic cloves, 1 onion, and carrot, and put everything in the oven at 200°F. After 8–10 hours, fish out all the solids. Pull the meat off the bones and reserve. Reduce the liquid over low heat for about five hours.

Put hominy and cal into a 3-gallon pot and cover with a few inches of water. Bring to a boil for 30 minutes, then turn off heat and let sit for an hour. Rinse hominy in a colander. Clean out the pot. Then put rinsed hominy back into the cleaned pot, cover with a few inches of water, bring to a boil for 30 minutes, and let it sit for an hour. Rinse thoroughly three times.

Add the meat along with jalapenos, chiles de arbol, the other onion, oregano, cumin, and chili powder. Simmer everything together until the flavors have married and it looks good enough to eat, around 90 minutes or so.

David Hammond writes two weekly columns, the Food Detective in the *Chicago Sun-Times* and "Omnivorous in Oak Park" in the Wednesday Journal. He's also a regular contributor of food-related segments to Chicago Public Radio and a founder/moderator of LTHForum.com, the Chicago-based culinary chat site.

# BORSCHT TWO WAYS
*from*
## DAVID KODESKI

For his first Soup & Bread, in 2009, David made both red borscht and white—a Polish variant that skips the beets in favor of a base made from fermented rye flour. Both were a big hit—and did you know red borscht is also known as a hangover cure? David notes that he decided to write the directions for each in the style his father had used when giving them to him, "with maybe a bit less backtracking."

## WHITE BORSCHT                         SERVES 8

### INGREDIENTS
- **4** cups fresh rye flour
- **8** cups lukewarm water
- **6–8** cups cool water
- garlic
- dried mushrooms
- vegetable stock
- **1** cup heavy cream

### PREPARATION

In a crock, mix together 4 cups of fresh rye flour and roughly 8 cups of lukewarm water. Cover and stick it someplace warm. The mixture will bubble. Once it has stopped bubbling and a mostly clear and brownish liquid (kvas) has formed, add 6–8 cups cool water, stir, and give it an hour or so to settle. Pour off the liquid and refrigerate. Some folks (my mother) would have added a few cloves of garlic to the liquid at this point and removed them before preparing the borscht.

Rehydrate some decent, flavorful, dark, dried mushrooms—Polish borowiki (Boletus edulis) are available online. Once they've been rehydrated, add them to the kvas. Pour in the liquid those mushrooms have been soaking in as well.

Sauté some minced garlic in a soup pot. Once it has become fragrant and started to color, add the kvas and mushroom mixture. Add enough vegetable stock to make it a nice amount without diminishing the tartness imparted by the kvas. Get it nice and hot.

Temper 1 cup (or more) of heavy cream with the hot liquid. Slowly add to the kvas/mushroom/stock mixture—you want more than anything at this point to avoid any curdling. Curdling will destroy this borscht. It's happened to me and made me most sad. At this point, my parents and grandparents would add Gravy Master to make it "nysse end brown"—I do not. Some folks add a touch of sugar at this point—I do not. Salt and fair amount of white pepper is good though.

Serve over boiled diced potatoes or with ushki—which is a recipe unto itself. Basically, they are tiny mushroom- and onion-filled pierogis that are distantly related to tortellini. I'll give you my babci's recipe if you make them and give me some.

## RED BEET BORSCHT                    SERVES 12-16

### INGREDIENTS
- **15** beets
- **6** cloves garlic, minced
- **1** tablespoon oil
- **8** cups vegetable stock
  water

### PREPARATION

In a crock (like the crock that comes in your large Crock-Pot)—place 6–7 beets cut into small wedges. Cover with lukewarm water. Place in warm spot. Because I keep my apartment "energy-efficient" cool I put the crock into the oven and leave the door cracked so the oven light stays on. Essentially you want to keep the crock about as warm as would be comfortable for yeast or a baby chick.

Cover and leave it alone for a week or so. The liquid will become tart. Some folks add a slice of sour rye bread to hasten the fermentation. If any mold forms, scrape it off the surface. It will not kill you. Once the liquid is sufficiently tart, pour off the liquid into a clean container.

In a soup pot, sauté the garlic. (I like to make a bit of a garlic paste using salt and the side of my butcher's knife). Once the garlic is fragrant and just beginning to color, add the beet liquid to the pot. Add vegetable stock. If possible you should make the stock yourself. Use your most flavorful recipe. (Or see page 189–190 for two options.) Simmer.

While all this is cooking, wrap remaining beets in aluminum foil and roast at 400°F for about 45 minutes or until soft. Let cool, then peel and cut into small dice. Add to soup pot and simmer a bit longer.

Serve with fresh dill and yogurt.

David Kodeski is a writer/performer and "pretty good cook" who has a website at truelifetales.com.

# PICKLE SOUP
### *from*
## TREA FOTIDZIS

Pickle soup is a Polish tradition, born of long winters when pickles were the most plentiful veggies to be had. It is utterly distinctive—tart and light, popping with the power of dill. Trea enlisted a friend to shred all the pickles for her, as the brine gives her a rash. Soup cooks with sensitive skin, consider yourselves warned.

## INGREDIENTS           SERVES 8

- **1** large jar Polish dill pickles, shredded and juice reserved
- **5-8** potatoes, peeled and diced
- **4-5** carrots, peeled and diced
- **3-4** celery stalks, diced
- **3-4** cloves of garlic, minced
- bunch of fresh dill, finely chopped
- **1** egg yolk
- **1** teaspoon of milk
- **1** teaspoon of olive oil
- salt and pepper to taste

## PREPARATION

Fill large pot with about 8 cups of water; boil the potatoes, carrots, and celery until tender. In a pan sauté minced garlic in teaspoon of olive oil. Add shredded pickles and sauté until softened. Dump softened pickles into pot of cooked veggies, add reserved pickle juice to taste. Season with salt and pepper. Beat egg yolk with a teaspoon of milk and drop into pot of soup. Add dill, stir it up, enjoy.

Trea Fotidzis is, in her words, "an old lady who lives in the bank."

# AVGOLEMONO
## (Lemon-Chicken Soup)
*from*
### HELEN TSATSOS

Helen prepared a pot of this essential Greek comfort food according to the recipe used by her mom and grandma. "My yiaya used to make this all the time," she says. "It is very easy and can be whipped up in a hurry with minimal effort. It is light but, thanks to the protein in the eggs, filling." If you're in the mood for something more substantial, she suggests following the lead of her foremothers and substituting lamb meatballs (kefthedes), artichoke bottoms, or stuffed grape leaves (domathes) for the shredded chicken.

### INGREDIENTS                    SERVES 8

- **8** cups chicken broth
- **3** medium eggs
- **½** cup rice
- juice from two lemons
- **1** cup cooked shredded chicken
- salt to taste

### PREPARATION

Bring chicken broth to a boil. Add rice or orzo, cover, and simmer for 20 minutes. Remove from heat.

In a blender, beat the three eggs until aerated, then slowly add the lemon juice to the eggs. With blender running, slowly add one cup of chicken broth. The constant blending is the secret to preventing curdling.

When the eggs and broth are well mixed, pour this mixture back into the remaining broth and rice. Add shredded chicken (or meatballs, artichokes, or stuffed grape leaves). Stir well over heat, but do not allow to boil. Salt to taste. Enjoy.

Helen Tsatsos is a jeweler by occupation, an architect by training, and a food lover by default.

# NEW ENGLAND CLAM CHOWDER
*from*
## MARAH EAKIN

What's more American than apple pie? Well, chowder, for one. Fish chowder was a common Friday night meal in early-American fishing communities along the Atlantic coast, and recipes for chowder turn up in regional cookbooks as far back as the 18th century. Clams, being cheap and plentiful along the eastern seaboard, took over the place of honor in the pot by the mid-19th century—Herman Melville devotes a whole chapter of *Moby Dick* to the stuff. While regional variations abound (Manhattan, Rhode Island), nothing is more evocative of home to a wandering New Englander than this classic creamy brew.

## INGREDIENTS                    SERVES 12

### CLAM BROTH
- **4** slices bacon, chopped
- olive oil
- **1** onion, chopped
- **2** garlic cloves, smashed
- **6** sprigs fresh thyme
- **1** bay leaf
- **16** littleneck clams, scrubbed well
- **½** lemon, juiced
- **½** cup white wine
- **3** cups water

### CHOWDER
- **2** tablespoons butter
- extra-virgin olive oil
- **4** slices bacon, chopped
- **1** onion, chopped
- **2** garlic cloves, minced
- leaves from 4 sprigs fresh thyme
- **¼** cup all-purpose flour
- **2** cups heavy cream
- **2** Idaho potatoes, peeled and diced
- salt and freshly ground black pepper
- **16** littleneck clams, scrubbed well
- **¼** cup chopped fresh flat-leaf parsley

## PREPARATION

**CLAM BROTH:** Put a large pot over medium heat, add the bacon and sauté until the fat is rendered and the bacon is browned, about 5 minutes. Remove the cooked bacon pieces from the pot and reserve them for something else. Add a glug of olive oil, the onion, garlic, thyme, and bay leaf and cook, stirring, until the vegetables are translucent, 3–5 minutes. Add the clams, lemon juice, white wine, and water and bring to a low boil. Reduce the heat, cover the pot, and simmer for 10–15 minutes to steam open the clams. Remove the clams from the pot, discarding any that don't open. Strain the broth into a bowl. Pull the clams out of their shells, chop them, and set them aside separately; discard the shells. Set the broth aside.

**CHOWDER:** Heat the butter and 1 tablespoon olive oil in a soup pot over medium heat. Add the bacon, onion, garlic, and thyme and cook until the bacon renders its fat and the vegetables are good and soft, 8 to 10 minutes. Dust the vegetables with flour and stir to coat everything well. Pour in the clam broth and bring to a boil. Add the cream and the potatoes, bring to a boil and boil hard for about 7 minutes, until the potatoes break down (this will help to thicken the soup and give it a good texture). Add the chopped clams and season with salt and pepper.

Now add the 16 clams in their shells. Cover and simmer to open the clams, about 10 minutes. Stir in the parsley and serve hot.

Marah Eakin is the Chicago city editor of the *A.V. Club* and claims to be heiress to the world's largest collection of antique and unique bedpans and urinals.

# KEWAUNEE INN CHEDDAR CHEESE AND BEER SOUP

*from*

## JOHN McKEVITT

Cheddar and beer—where else could this soup originate but Wisconsin? It's inspired by the Kewaunee Inn, a 100-year-old hotel on the shores of Lake Michigan that claims to be the oldest operating haunted inn in the midwest. But you don't have to see ghosts to appreciate the otherworldly quality of this rich, smooth soup. If you've never been a big cheese soup fan, this could make you a believer.

### INGREDIENTS

SERVES 12

- ¾ cup unsalted butter
- ¾ cup minced onions
- ⅓ cup thinly sliced mushrooms
- ¼ cup rough-cut celery
- 2 tablespoons minced fresh garlic
- ¾ cup all-purpose flour
- 12 cups chicken stock
- 1 cup dark beer
- 2 pounds grated cheddar cheese
- 1½ teaspoons dry mustard
- 1 cup heavy cream, hot
  Tabasco sauce, as needed
  Worcestershire sauce, as needed
  salt
  ground white pepper

### PREPARATION

In a large soup pot heat the butter over medium heat. Sweat the onions, mushrooms, celery, and garlic until the onions are translucent. Add the flour and cook to make a blond roux, about 12–14 minutes, whisking constantly to work out any lumps. Add the stock gradually, continuing to whisk. Simmer 45 minutes, or until the soup has a good flavor and velvety texture. Strain through a fine mesh sieve. The soup is now ready to finish, or may be refrigerated for later use.

Return the soup to a simmer. Add the beer and the cheese and continue to heat gently until the cheese melts. Do not boil.

Blend the dry mustard with enough water to make a paste. Add the mustard mixture and the cream and bring the soup back to a simmer. Adjust the

# Bully for Booyah

The Back Bay may love its chowder, but up in Green Bay, booyah is the soup du jour. A popular regional specialty, this thick stew is unknown outside the upper midwest, but pass through any small town between Green Bay and Saint Paul and you'll probably see the signs: "Booyah Today."

Both a soup and a ritual, booyah is believed to have originated with the Belgian Walloons who settled around Green Bay in the 19th century. The name's a devolution from the French verb *bouiller,* or "to boil." Minnesotans drop the *h,* but over the border the concept remains the same. Made of chicken—and maybe beef, or pork, or all three—mixed with vegetables and seasoned with allspice and paprika, it's cooked in vast kettles outdoors over an open fire for many, many hours, until the veggies are disintegrating and the meat is in shreds.

"You can't make a little bit of booyah," says Cathy Lambrecht, vice president of the Greater Midwest Foodways Alliance. "It's one of those things there's so many ingredients that even if you only use a little bit of each, you wind up with a ton of soup." A booyah recipe cited by Nelson Algren, unlikely author of the WPA's "America Eats" guide to the Midwest, calls for 30 pounds of oxtail, "four fat hens," and a peck each (eight dry quarts) of kohlrabi, rutabaga, carrots, and potatoes.

Needless to say, as it involves getting up early, and lighting fires, and (often) drinking beer, booyah tends to be a guy thing. Teams of men may take turns coaxing the soup along, stoking the fire and stirring the pot (sometimes with a canoe paddle) for hours on end, or even overnight. But, like a fish fry, or the making of the burgoo and Brunswick stews popular farther south, booyah is above all a communal event—a popular fundraiser for small town churches, schools, and volunteer fire departments. When the cooking's done and the beer's been drunk, the whole community can partake, pitching in a few dollars for a bowl with oyster crackers or a quart to take home, priced by the ladle.

---

consistency with stock as desired. Season with the Tabasco, Worcestershire, salt, and pepper as desired.

Serve in heated bowls or cups with rye croutons.

John McKevitt is an aging social activist fascinated by performing arts, cooking, and those interesting people on either end of the bell curve of life.

# GUMBO—BRIDGEPORT STYLE
*from*
## CHUCK SUDO

The state dish of Louisiana, gumbo is infinitely variable: Creole varieties build off a base of shrimp and other seafood. More Cajun influenced versions, like this one, rely on meat and sausage. Most get their characteristic gummy consistency from okra, slow-simmered to mitigate its oddly mucilaginous texture, though some recipes substitute filé—a powder of ground sassafras leaves—to similar effect. Chuck's recipe (which he credits to his neighborhood on Chicago's south side) teams okra with a dark, smoky roux to create a strong foundation for the equally strong flavors of this ultra satisfying dish.

## INGREDIENTS                    SERVES 8–12

- **2** pounds chicken, chopped
- **1** pound smoked sausage, sliced
- **1** cup rendered chicken fat
- **2** cups flour
- **1** red bell pepper, diced
- **1** small yellow onion, diced
- **1** cup okra, sliced
- **1** clove garlic, minced
- **1** tablespoon Creole seasoning
- **1** teaspoon smoked paprika
- **1** teaspoon sea salt
- **1** teaspoon dried thyme
- **1** bay leaf
- **8–10** cups chicken stock

## PREPARATION

In a large pan, sauté the chicken and smoked sausage on high heat; remove from pan and set aside. Add the rendered chicken fat to the pan and warm until just bubbling. Sift flour into pan and whisk until mixed with the chicken fat and foaming. Reduce heat to medium and stir regularly, until the roux turns mahogany-colored, or about an hour, then add garlic, onion, bell pepper, okra, and seasonings and cook until soft (2–3 minutes).

Bring chicken stock to a boil in a large stock pot, then reduce heat, add vegetables and roux from pan, plus bay leaf, and simmer about 45–60 minutes. Add chicken and smoked sausage and simmer an additional 15–25 minutes. Serve over rice.

Chuck Sudo is the editor in chief of Chicagoist.com and "the last of the hard-core troubadours."

# FREE-RANGE BREAD

*from*

## HUGH AMANO

Flour. Water. Salt. This is the most fundamental bread recipe around, and one that, despite the time commitment, and the unpredictability of sourdough starter, is actually not all that hard to execute—and execute well. Here it is, in Hugh's own words.

**INGREDIENTS**
   flour
   water
   salt

**PREPARATION**

To capture airborne yeast, combine a couple of tablespoons of flour with a couple of tablespoons of water. I use filtered water, incidentally—have you smelled tap water lately? There is so much chlorine in it I fear it won't give the tiny yeast a fighting chance to breed.

So, knead the dough a bit, then put it in a bowl, cover it with a damp towel, and let it hang out in a warm place. After a couple of days there will be a bit of a crust on the dough. Peel that off and discard it. There should be some evidence, however slight, of yeast production in the form of tiny bubbles or holes in the dough. Refresh the starter by adding another couple tablespoons of flour and water and repeat the process, again checking progress in a couple of days. Then do it again.

By the third refreshment there should be ample evidence of yeast. At this point, you should have a small bit of starter, weighing maybe 6 ounces or so, depending on how much crust had to be thrown out. Reserve a bit of this starter in a jar in the fridge, for next time.

To the rest of the starter add about 8 ounces (approximately 2 cups) of bread flour, and enough water to make a firm dough that is slightly tacky to the touch, but not sticky. Knead for about 15 minutes and let rise until about doubled in size. Punch down, then knead in about 2 teaspoons of salt and just enough additional flour so it's not super sticky. Shape bread into long loaves or rounds. Let rise until doubled in size again, then bake in a 425°F oven until done, maybe 20–25 minutes. The loaves will sound hollow when tapped, and the internal temperature will be around 190–200°F. Cool. Eat.

Hugh Amano is a chef, writer, and general food lover living in Chicago who wants people to return to cooking. His writing on food can be seen at foodonthedole. blogspot.com.

# CHAPTER TWO

# Soup for Swapping

$\mathcal{H}$'s hard to make soup for one.

That's obvious, sure. But Knox Gardner has turned that simple truth into a movement.

In 1999, Knox, tired of having to repeat meals to finish off a pot of soup, called a couple of friends and asked them to come over. Bring your own homemade soup parceled out into small containers, he said. He'd been playing a lot of Pit—the stock-trading card game—and envisioned some friendly horse trading around the dining room table: I'll give you two corn chowders for one of those minestrones...

The trading turned out to be bit more free-form than that, but in the years that followed, Soup Swap Day became a winter tradition for his circle. Then when Knox moved from Seattle to Boston, his friends decided they didn't need him to stoke the fire. Instead, they coordinated. East coast and west both held a swap on the same day—and National Soup Swap Day was born.

Now hundreds of swappers celebrate National Soup Swap Day in January, posting recipes, video testimonials, and news of swaps scheduled nationwide to Knox's website, soupswap.com—not to mention links to the press coverage that's followed everywhere from *USA Today* to the *Siskiyou Daily News*.

"Soup is such a weird food," says Knox, who's since moved back to Seattle. "It's tied very much to comfort and tradition and community and sharing. I never thought about it before I started this thing, but now for sure I get it." No one has to be a slave to his schedule, he adds. Busy on National Soup Swap Day? "Swap when you can!"

On his website, Knox lays out the guidelines for a successful swap. Get some friends—preferably ones who like soup—and pick a place to swap. Ask each person to bring six quarts of soup divided into quart-size servings (say, freezer bags or yogurt containers) labeled with the ingredients. If six quarts seems onerous, shoot for four, or, as my friend Bonnie did when she threw a swap, a tidy three. Everyone draws a number, and you go around the group in order taking turns picking soups till everything's been taken.

Knox says the best part is before the swapping starts, when every swapper steps up to say a little something about his or her soup.

"In Seattle we'll have 20 soups," he says. "And we have people who come to our soup swap who have never met, ever—but they get up in front of this room of people and they say, 'I made this soup and it's my grandma's recipe and it has this and that, or that'—and it's just awesome, it's a really powerful moment."

Serious swappers can get competitive. Knox says he's heard tall tales about soups made from grain hand-washed by Swedish virgins and ancient family recipes passed in secret down through the generations.

But it's all in good fun—and sometimes surprising connections are made. After Knox mentioned on his site that he and his male partner were working on adopting a baby, he got an email from a fellow swapper in rural Ohio. "She's very conservative, and she runs a blog, all about Jesus, and she and her husband have adopted five Russian children," Knox said. "And she sent us a note, and it just started this three-month-long exchange that was just awesome—this conversation about adoption with this woman who I would never have met otherwise, and who I thought, from her blog, would be really against me and my partner adopting."

Soup swaps have been slow to catch on in big cities like New York and Chicago, but according to Knox they're hot in smaller communities—something he attributes to stronger traditions of home cooking and church suppers. And the country real estate can't hurt—it's hard to host a swap in a studio apartment.

Whatever the reason, my experience supports Knox's generalization: I wanted to swap some soup for "research," but attempts to find a swap in the Chicago area were fruitless, and, yes, my own apartment is tiny. I finally convinced Bonnie to do the honors.

On a chilly February Sunday two dozen friends and neighbors—one from across the hall—descended on the duplex apartment Bonnie shares with her husband, Ted, two children, and two cats. It had been a rough week: Ted had just lost his job and Bonnie was only working part-time, but she was determined to put a positive spin on their predicament: "More time for cooking—and swapping!" she said, brandishing a wooden spoon.

Bonnie made a cream of artichoke soup from the first edition of the *Soup & Bread Cookbook* (the recipe's reprinted here on page 168). When she ran it through the blender, it turned a distressing shade of khaki, so she freestyled, tossing in bits of parsley till it developed an enticing shade of green.

"Making this soup taught me that I could riff on a recipe," she said when she introduced her soup, adding that she made it for Ted, who had never eaten an artichoke until they met.

The artichoke soup shared a crowded table with tubs and jars and ziplock bags full of wild mushroom, hot and sour, chicken tortilla, and two versions of butternut squash soup. Some were fancy—Molly, a former coworker of Bonnie's, accessorized each container of her pumpkin soup with a little baggie of Parmesan and a small green apple, to be sprinkled and sliced, respectively, on top. (See page 47 for Molly's own soup story.) Jessica, a journalist, apologized for the no-frills look of her vegan split pea soup, which she'd delivered in plastic tubs swiped from the hot bar at Whole Foods.

Kate, Ted's sister, brought three different soups, all whipped up by her Polish babysitter—pickle soup, white borscht, and a chicken and split pea concoction called "zupka," which simply means "soup." Kate's presentation was met with sighs, the babysitter's soup skills being, apparently, the stuff of neighborhood legend.

In three lightning rounds it was all gone: First the wild mushroom, then the hot and sour, the onion, and the chicken tortilla (with chips, cheese, and cilantro on the side). Jessica's split pea was one of the last to go. "Oh, wait! Look!" she quipped to her neighbor. "Someone's touching it!"

Later I asked Guy and Kristin—an actor/meat eater and a photographer/vegetarian—how they prepared for their first swap. The veggie butternut squash with jalapeno they supplied was a favorite recipe and a no-brainer, they said. But they engaged in "an embarrassingly long discussion on the merits of a ziplock bag (Kristin) versus a firm container (Guy)." Guy won, and Kristin gussied the Tupperware up with kitchen twine and cards inked with the recipe.

Next time, said Bonnie, "I'm giving out door prizes—like, for most colorful soup and best packaging."

When I asked Knox Gardner what he got out of being the soup swap mastermind, he replied, "I get soup in my freezer, that's about it,"—though he said—was thinking of maybe selling Soup Swap aprons online to at least cover the cost of his server. "That, and warm and fuzzy feelings."

Bonnie agreed that hosting a swap was an end in itself. A few days after the swap she and Ted ate their friend Fran's spinach soup for lunch together, at home, without children. "We were really happy—it's the most we've laughed in a long time," she said. "There's certainly some joy to be had in not working."

# MINESTRONE
*from*
## CAMILLE SEVERINO

The great thing about minestrone, points out Camille, is that it can absorb whatever you like, or whatever you've got lying around. For vegetables she suggests carrots, celery, zucchini, yellow squash, and green beans, but leafy greens like spinach and escarole are also good, and corn and okra can give it a southern flair. For a twist, she also suggests subbing black beans for the kidney beans.

### INGREDIENTS

SERVES 8–12

- **2** tablespoons olive oil
- **1** yellow onion, chopped
- **3-4** cloves of garlic, minced
- **4** cups (or so) of cut-up vegetables, whatever you like (can be frozen)
- water
- **1** can garbanzo beans
- **1** can red kidney beans
- salt and pepper
- bay leaf
- **2** cups cooked ditalini pasta
- grated Romano cheese

### PREPARATION

Sauté onion and garlic in olive oil in large pot until soft, over medium heat. Add your vegetables and cover with water. Salt and pepper to taste. Pop in the bay leaf and let cook until the vegetables are soft. Then add your beans, simmer for another half an hour, add cooked pasta and grated cheese. Remove bay leaf. Eat. Easy peasy.

Camille Severino is a fan of cooking soup and an even bigger fan of feeding people; she organizes the annual Jambalaya Cookoff at FitzGerald's Nightclub in Berwyn, Illinois.

# GILLS' BOUNTIFUL VEGETABLE SOUP
*from*
## SHEILA SACHS

Bountiful for sure, and bursting with basil—this vegetable soup has a Mediterranean kick thanks to the pesto topping, which fancifies it as well. It was prepared by Sheila for Soup & Bread in honor of our Kickstarter donors Jim and Sue Gill, whose generous contribution helped fund the publication of the first edition of our cookbook. Thanks Gills!

## INGREDIENTS                    SERVES 10

### SOUP
- **2** tablespoons olive oil
- **2** medium onions, diced
- **2** medium carrots, sliced into discs
- **1** medium rib celery, diced
- **2** cloves garlic, minced
- **10** cups stock, vegetable or chicken
- **4** medium new potatoes, cut into ½-inch cubes
- **1** 14-ounce can diced tomatoes or 2 large tomatoes, peeled, seeded, and chopped
- **¼** teaspoon summer savory (or ⅛ teaspoon marjoram and ⅛ teaspoon thyme)
- salt and fresh ground black pepper
- **1** medium zucchini, cut into ¼-inch cubes
- **1** medium yellow squash, cut into ¼-inch cubes
- **2** ears corn, kernels cut from cob (or 1½ cups frozen)
- **¼** pound green beans, trimmed and cut into 1-inch lengths
- **½** cup elbow macaroni
- **½** cup fresh parsley, chopped
- **¼** cup fresh basil, chopped

### BASIL PESTO                    MAKES ABOUT 2 CUPS
- **2** cups fresh basil leaves
- **2** cloves garlic
- **½** cup olive oil
- **½** teaspoon salt
- **½** cup Parmesan cheese
- **¼** cup pine nuts, toasted

## PREPARATION

SOUP: Heat oil in a large soup pot. Add onions, carrots, and celery. Sauté until vegetables soften, about 5 minutes. Add garlic and sauté until fragrant, about 1 minute. Add stock, bring to a simmer, and simmer 1–2 minutes.

With the soup base at a simmer, add potatoes, tomatoes, summer savory; salt to taste and simmer for 30 minutes. Add squashes, corn, and beans and simmer 5 minutes. Add macaroni and simmer until pasta is done, about 10 minutes. Stir in parsley and basil. Season with additional salt, if necessary, and pepper to taste. Serve with basil pesto dollop.

PESTO: Puree basil and garlic with olive oil in a food processor. Blend in salt, cheese and nuts. (This will yield more than you'll need, but pesto can be frozen and will keep in the refrigerator for up to three weeks.)

Jim, Sue, Lucy, and Ella Gill live in Oak Park, IL, where Jim presides over a bountiful vegetable garden.

Sheila Sachs is a graphic designer living in Chicago. She designed this book you are holding.

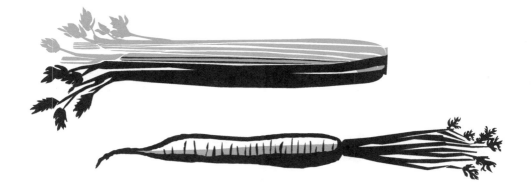

# CREAM OF MUSHROOM SOUP
*from*
## KNOX GARDNER

Knox not only graciously answered all my questions about soup swaps when I contacted him out of the blue, he also whipped up this savory and oh-so-smooth cream of mushroom soup for Soup & Bread night in Seattle. The recipe is adapted from *S.O.U.P.S.: Seattle's Own Undeniably Perfect Soups*, by Michael Congdon, chef at that city's Hopvine pub.

**INGREDIENTS**                SERVES 12

- **1** large baking potato
- **4** tablespoons unsalted butter
- **1** tablespoon truffle oil
- **1** large yellow onion, thinly sliced
- **1-2** shallots
- **1-2** cloves of garlic
- **¾** cup cream sherry
- **1½** pounds white mushrooms, chopped
- **4** cups vegetable stock
  black peppercorns
  salt
- **4** bay leaves
- **2** cups cream
  several sprigs of thyme

## PREPARATION

Bake potato at 500°F for 30–45 minutes or microwave. When a fork or knife can be inserted smoothly, it is done. Let cool.

Melt the butter in a large stock pan, and add the truffle oil. Add the garlic, shallots, and onions, stirring occasionally until they begin to caramelize—this could take as long as 20 minutes. When the onions are soft, gooey, and brown, add ¼ cup of the sherry and make sure to get all the tasty bits that may be stuck at the bottom of the pan.

Now add the mushrooms and the rest of the sherry. Cover for 5–10 minutes to let the mushrooms reduce.

Add 2 cups of the stock, along with 1 teaspoon peppercorns, 1 teaspoon salt, and the bay leaves. Cook for 30 minutes or until all the ingredients are soft.

In batches, puree the mushroom and onion mix while adding chunks of the potato for more structure, putting the resulting mix into a clean pot if possible. Adding only a few ladles at a time to a blender or food processor (too much and you'll end up with hot soup all over your kitchen!), alternate between the hot mushroom mixture and pieces of potatoes with additional stock.

Once the mushrooms, potatoes, and stock have been blended together (and you may have two pots going now) add the 2 cups of cream along with a fistful of fresh, chopped thyme. Bring to a simmer and adjust the taste with salt and pepper.

Ideally, you'd chill this soup for a day or two for the flavor to develop, but if you don't have time, it ought to still taste delicious.

As with all cream soups, it's important to reheat slowly and gently. Present with a drop or two of truffle oil.

Knox Gardner lives in Seattle and has been swapping soup since 1999.

# WEST TOWN TAVERN
# WILD MUSHROOM CHOWDER
*from*
## SUSAN GOSS

Chef Susan Goss says this is probably the heartiest of the soups in regular rotation at the cozy Chicago restaurant she owns with her husband, Drew. They may call it a tavern, but the food is far from pub grub. This soup is rich and sophisticated on its own, but the crunchy, funky blue cheese croutons kick it to a new level entirely. (For more of Susan's thoughts on soup see page 162.)

## INGREDIENTS                    SERVES 6

### SOUP

- **2** tablespoons canola oil
- **1** large yellow onion, peeled, finely chopped
- **4** cups chopped mixed mushrooms (cremini, shiitake, oyster and the like)
- **1½** cups carrot, small dice
- **2⅓** cups peeled potato, small dice
- **3** cloves garlic, peeled, smashed, minced (about 1 tablespoon)
- **½** cup dry sherry
- **5⅓** cups water or vegetable stock
- **2** large bay leaves
- **4** sprigs fresh thyme
- **1⅓** cups heavy cream
  kosher salt, to taste
  ground black pepper, to taste
- **2** tablespoons Worcestershire sauce
- **1** teaspoon bottled hot sauce
- **2** tablespoons fresh thyme leaves, minced

### BLUE CHEESE CROUTONS        MAKES ABOUT 2 CUPS

- **2** cups French bread cubes, about 1 inch by 1 inch
- **4** tablespoons unsalted butter
- **3** ounces blue cheese, crumbled

## PREPARATION

CROUTONS: In a small saucepan over low heat, combine the butter and cheese. Melt the butter and cheese, stirring occasionally until smooth. Pour butter mixture over bread cubes and toss gently to mix.

Spread bread cubes onto a cookie sheet and separate as much as possible. Scrape any remaining butter mixture over cubes.

Bake bread cubes for 7 minutes in a 350°F oven. Turn gently with a spatula and bake until golden brown and crisp, about 5 more minutes. Let croutons cool completely before using.

Store croutons covered at room temperature up to 24 hours.

SOUP: In a large saucepan over medium heat, heat the oil and sauté the onion until tender and browned, about 7 minutes. Add the mushrooms, cover the pan and lower the heat. Steam the mushrooms for 5 minutes until they begin to give up their juices. Uncover the pan, raise the heat to medium, and sauté the mushrooms until they are tender, another 7–10 minutes. Add the carrots, potatoes, and garlic and stir well. Add the sherry and bring to a boil. Boil until sherry reduces to a glaze, about 2–3 minutes.

Add the water. Tie the bay leaves and thyme sprigs together and add to the saucepan. Bring to a boil, reduce the heat to medium-low and simmer the soup until the potatoes and carrots are tender, about 20 minutes. Remove and discard the bay leaves and thyme sprigs.

Add the cream and return the soup to a boil. Reduce the heat to medium and simmer until the cream is slightly reduced, about 10 minutes more. Season the soup with salt and pepper and stir in the Worcestershire, hot sauce, and minced thyme.

If desired, transfer 1 cup of soup to a blender and puree. Return puree to the saucepan and stir well. Serve garnished with blue cheese croutons.

Susan Goss is chef and co-owner of Chicago's West Town Tavern. She's the author of *West Town Tavern: Contemporary Comfort Food*, published in December 2010.

# BUTTERNUT AND ACORN SQUASH SOUP
*from*
## JACK NEWELL

Jack adapted this from a recipe in Eric Ripert and Michael Ruhlman's book *A Return to Cooking*, which Jack describes as "half cookbook, half L.L. Bean magazine starring Eric Ripert doing different rustic, food-related things, all the while looking fabulous." It's a great showcase for the rich, pure flavors of the squash, and very easy to prepare.

**INGREDIENTS**          SERVES 8

- **6** tablespoons unsalted butter
- **1** cup sliced yellow onion
- **2** cups peeled and diced acorn squash
- **2** cups peeled and diced butternut squash
- fine sea salt
- fresh ground white pepper (fresh and white are very important here)
- **5** cups chicken stock
- **1** cup heavy cream
- **3** thyme sprigs
- **3** ounces sharp cheddar cheese
- **1** nutmeg—for grating
- honey (optional)
- cayenne (optional)
- minced ginger (optional)

**PREPARATION**

Melt 2 tablespoons butter in a large pot over medium heat. Add the onions and cook until translucent, about 3 minutes. Add squash and sauté until softened, about 10 minutes.

Cover with the chicken stock and bring to a simmer, cook until squash is tender, about 30 minutes.

Decant soup into a food processor or blender and puree until satiny-smooth, or use an immersion blender to puree in the pot. If you like, pass soup through a mesh sieve to remove any particulate matter. Return soup to pot. Add cream and remaining 4 tablespoons of butter. Bring to a simmer.

Wrap the thyme in cheesecloth and tie the package with the string. Add to the simmering soup and let it infuse for 10 minutes. Remove the thyme. Add the cheese, grated nutmeg, a dollop of honey and a dash of cayenne (if using), plus salt and pepper to taste. Serve.

Jack Newell is a filmmaker living and working in Chicago. He teaches directing at Columbia College Chicago.

# GREEN CURRIED
# BUTTERNUT SQUASH SOUP
*from*
## JILL BARRON

Chef Jill Barron does strange and wonderful things with ostensibly simple vegetarian food, and this soup was no exception. Right off the bat, the color upends your preconceptions—you hear "squash" and the last thing you expect is pale pea-green soup. Then, the unassuming color sets you up to expect something mild, but it's not—at all. The spice sneaks up on you, but once arrived, it provides a potent blast of flavor.

## INGREDIENTS

SERVES 8

### SOUP

- 1 tablespoon olive oil
- 1 onion, peeled and diced
- 1 large butternut squash, seeded and roasted
- 4 cups vegetable stock
- 1 tablespoon brown sugar
- 1 tablespoon salt

### GREEN CURRY

- 1 stalk of lemongrass, chopped
- 1 Serrano chili
- 1 shallot
- 5 cloves garlic
- 2 inches fresh ginger, peeled and sliced
- ½ bunch cilantro, washed and chopped (stems are OK)
- ½ cup basil leaves
- ½ teaspoon cumin
- ½ teaspoon black pepper
- ½ teaspoon coriander
- 1 tablespoon soy sauce
- ½ teaspoon salt
- 2 tablespoons lime juice
- 1 teaspoon honey
- 1 can coconut milk

## PREPARATION

SOUP: In a large stockpot over medium heat, sauté onion in olive oil until soft and fragrant. Scoop out squash and add to pot, along with stock, sugar, and salt. Cook until soft, then add 1 cup green curry. Puree with immersion blender and serve, garnished with a lime wedge.

CURRY: Puree all together in blender till smooth.

Jill Barron is chef/owner of Mana Food Bar in Chicago.

# WAYWARD CATHOLIC CHICKEN SOUP
*from*
## KERRI HARROP

Kerri brought this chicken soup to our first Soup & Bread in Seattle, which went down on January 30, 2011, at the Funhouse, a punk-rock bar near Seattle Center. Kerri turned out to be one of those people who knows everyone in town—she knew three of the other soup cooks that night, though the three had never met each other. As for her soup, she says: "Little old Jewish ladies get all the props for good chicken soup, but I grew up eating bowls of my Nana's Irish-Catholic version, which gets its designation by the omission of matzoh balls and the addition of crackers. Very Body of Christ, without all the Latin."

### INGREDIENTS

SERVES 10

- **1** whole chicken
- **1** sweet onion
- **4–5** stalks of celery
- **4–5** nice looking carrots
- **1–2** cloves of garlic
  coarse sea salt and fresh ground pepper
  olive oil
  egg noodles
  saltine crackers

### PREPARATION

First, you gotta roast a chicken for dinner, one or two days before you make soup. I like to rub the bird with olive oil and a secret blend of herbs and spices, stick a lemon (halved) in its cavity, and stuff garlic under its skin. After you have dinner, put the leftovers in the fridge, including all the bones.

The next day, remove the meat from the bird's cold carcass and make some stock. (See page 192 for a recipe.) Save the meat and put it back in the fridge.

Now, the soup: Chop the onion up nicely, and sauté it in some olive oil. The pot you are using to cook it is your soup pot, so make sure it is big enough. Once the onion is getting soft and pretty, throw in a clove or two of minced garlic. Don't let it get too brown.

While this is going on, you should have been getting your chicken meat ready. How you do that is up to you. If you like it shredded, go for it. If you like chunks, get chopping. Mix it up both ways if you want.

Add the meat to your onion and garlic, and give it a little stir. The chicken is already cooked, so don't overdo it. Once everything has gotten to know each other, throw in your chicken stock. (If you don't have enough, you can use some store-bought—just make sure it isn't gross. Spend the extra money.)

Reduce the heat and cover. Now, chop up your celery and carrots and throw that veg in the pot. Do you like other stuff in your chicken soup? Go ahead and add it. Sometimes fresh green beans are lovely, or maybe some English peas. Have a tomato that is about to go south? It can go in the pot, no big whoop.

Add salt and pepper. Don't be stingy. Now, just let it simmer all day. Hopefully you have a baguette on hand, so you can dunk it in and taste the soup when the smell is just driving you crazy with hunger.

There are a few schools of thought when it comes to adding noodles. Me, I wait until the last half hour or so. The longer those noodles are in the soup, the more they will soak up the broth. They will expand, and that is not a bad thing, but I like them a little more controlled.

Whatever you do, make sure you boil the noodles first in a separate pot. If you just throw in dry noodles, the soup will be too starchy. Don't like noodles? Try rice! Want your soup to be more like a stew? Use potatoes! Feeling weird? Throw in a yam, or some squash. Just make sure you boil all this stuff to at least al dente before you add it.

Starving? Have a bowl of soup. Crumble up some saltines on top—it is delicious. If you are feeling fancy, you can sprinkle some chopped parsley on top. Use the Italian version—it is way better. Drink some red wine with it. Almost everything is better with red wine. My Nana would agree.

Seattle native Kerri Harrop is a longtime DJ/writer/community activist/ blabbermouth who "loves to cook good food for nice humans and does not trust anyone who says they don't like Led Zeppelin."

# TANGY CHICKEN TORTILLA SOUP

*from*

## HELEN ROSNER

I'm not sure if it's an effect of Rick Bayless winning *Top Chef Masters* or what, but 2010 saw an inordinate number of chicken tortilla soups pass through the Soup & Bread pots. This was one of two chicken tortilla soups at our event at the Bell House, in Brooklyn. In her note to me Helen apologized for using so many store-bought elements—noting that she'd planned to cook from scratch but ran out of time. To which I say, "No shame in store-bought." Aspirations aside, most of us aren't living in an Alice Waters paradise—and besides, her soup was really good. It's comforting, as chicken soup should be, but with a sophisticated degree of heat and pizzazz.

**INGREDIENTS**                    SERVES 8-10

- **4** tablespoons olive oil
- **6** cloves garlic, minced
- **1** small jalapeno, seeds and ribs removed, minced
- **1** store-bought rotisserie chicken, skin discarded and meat coarsely shredded (about 3 cups)—keep the carcass to make stock!
- **8** cups chicken stock
- **1** 14-ounce can diced tomatoes (or, if it's summer, fresh tomatoes: skinned, seeded, and diced, juice reserved)
  pinch cumin
  pinch onion powder (not onion salt)
- **2** tablespoons salt
  juice of 4 limes (about ½ cup)
- **1** teaspoon hot sauce*
- **1** teaspoon white wine vinegar

GARNISH

  tortilla chips
  diced avocado
  minced cilantro
  sour cream
  lime wedges

## PREPARATION

Heat the oil in a large, heavy-bottomed pot over medium-low heat. Add the garlic and sauté until fragrant, about 20–30 seconds. Add the minced jalapeno and sauté another 10–15 seconds. Dump in the shredded chicken and incorporate the garlic/pepper mixture; turn up the heat to medium. Folding constantly, sauté until the garlic is just barely browning, then remove from the pot and reserve.

Combine the chicken stock, tomatoes, spices, salt, and lime juice in the same pot and heat until gently simmering. Add the lime juice and hot sauce and return the pot to a simmer, skimming any foam. Stir in the reserved chicken/garlic/chili mixture. Simmer for 10 minutes, or until the tomatoes and chicken have slightly disintegrated.

While the soup is cooking, prepare the garnishes: Dice avocado (toss it with lime juice to keep it from browning), mince cilantro, slice limes into wedges, crush your tortilla chips, whatever is to your taste. (If you're swapping, consider wrapping the garnish up in little packages for added swap-peal.)

Just before serving, remove the soup from the heat and stir in the white wine vinegar. To serve, I prefer to fill the bowls with the tortilla chips first, then the soup, then the other garnishes, but it's all the same in the end.

*A note on hot sauce: I used Sriracha, which I use for everything. You could of course substitute something more tortilla-appropriate like Cholula, but the key is a sauce that's as much about flavor as heat. Even if you like things spicy, I'd advise against adding extra hot sauce to the cooking soup to taste—the broth should be clear and almost delicate, with a balance among the meaty chicken, sour lime, sweet tomato, and hot sauce. (This is basically a kluged Mexican-style tom yum.) Serve extra hot sauce with the garnish and add to taste.

Helen Rosner is the web editor for *Saveur* magazine. She was the founding editor of the blog Grub Street Chicago, an editor of Grub Street New York, and the books editor for EatMeDaily.com She lives in New York, where she doesn't cook nearly as often as she'd like to.

# SPLIT PEA SOUP
# WITH BLACK FOREST HAM

*from*

## AMY LOMBARDI

Amy made this surprisingly low-fat soup twice during the 2009 Soup & Bread season. It is super satisfying, mildly infused with the characteristic smokiness of ham but retaining more of the pure flavor of the protein-rich peas. Says Amy, "I'm not a fan of an overwhelmingly hammy flavor in this soup which is one reason I don't use a hock. Plus, parts that release that kind of flavor also render too much fat, which gives me a tummy ache and takes over the whole soup. I like a lighter version, where the peas and carrots have equal billing with the pork."

**INGREDIENTS**                     SERVES 6

| | |
|---|---|
| 2 | tablespoons olive oil |
| 2 | cups chopped carrots (bite-size pieces) |
| 1-1½ | cups Black Forest ham (also chopped into bite-size niblets) |
| 2–3 | medium garlic cloves (minced) |
| 1 | pound bag dry split peas |
| 1 | bay leaf |
| 1 | teaspoon thyme (optional) |
| 1 | tablespoon unsalted butter |
| 10 | cups water (hold 2 in reserve) |
| | sea salt and fresh ground pepper |

**PREPARATION**

Strain and rinse peas. Dig around and remove any stones or unsightly shells.

Heat a large soup pot or Dutch oven to medium low and add olive oil. Add carrots, ham, and garlic and cook slowly, about 7–10 minutes, stirring a bit here and there. Lower heat if any browning occurs.

Turn heat up to medium high, add peas, bay leaf, thyme, butter, and 8 cups water. Stir (from the bottom) and cook for 30–40 minutes, occasionally giving a turn (again, from the bottom), Take note of the soup's consistency; the peas should be starting to absorb the water, allowing the soup to thicken. If this is not happening, cook for another 10 minutes uncovered, then stir and proceed to next step.

Turn heat down to low, add 1 teaspoon sea salt, stir, cover, and cook for 15 minutes. Soup should have a few inches of water on top, but will thicken when stirred. If it seems too thick, add more water (¼ cup at a time) and cook for another 10 minutes. Remove bay leaf, add fresh ground pepper to taste. Serve with sliced, toasted ciabatta.

Amy Lombardi lives in Austin, TX with her dog Arthur, works in the music Industry and teaches at community college.

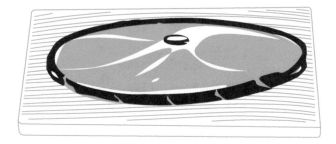

# HUMMUS SOUP
*from*
## MICHAEL GEBERT

The humble vegetarian trappings of this soup are deceptive; it's built on a smoky bacon stock and finished with a crispy garnish of fried Spanish ham. It's adapted from Anya von Bremzen's *The New Spanish Table* and Mike dished it up at Soup & Bread in 2009. Says he, "The underlying concept is so simple: It's basically making any split pea soup recipe with chickpeas instead of split peas. I make soup by feel—if you need more precision than below, check out her original recipe."

## INGREDIENTS                    SERVES 12

- **1** medium onion, chopped
- **1** leek, white part sliced
- **1** carrot, diced
- **3** cloves of garlic, chopped
- **6–8** cups of water
- **1** hunk of bacon or ham or salt pork or smoked ham hock or any flavorful hunk of pork; the more flavor it has, the better your soup will be, so choose wisely.
- **2** 15-ounce cans of chickpeas, with most but not all of their liquid poured off
  olive oil
  smoked paprika
  jamon iberico (or serrano)

## PREPARATION

Put onion (including discarded tops), carrot, leek, and garlic in stockpot with a little olive oil, and fry fairly low for 2–3 minutes, then cover pot and cook 5–7 minutes more.

Add water and the hunk of pork. Let simmer for a couple of hours, partly covered, until it makes a nice stock.

Meanwhile, heat ¼ cup of olive oil in a pan over low heat till almost hot. Remove from heat and sprinkle 1 heaping teaspoon of smoked paprika into it. Let sit for 45 minutes, then pour off oil into small bowl or jar, leaving paprika behind.

Add chickpeas to stock, and let simmer for another hour.

Remove pork and save for at least one more use. Season to taste—salt and pepper only. If it needs sharpening, give it a little slug of sherry vinegar. But be sparing! If you can taste the vinegar, you've used too much.

Fry a couple of slices of jamon iberico or serrano in a pan till they just start to crisp up. Remove and cut into ¼-inch squares. They will continue crisping after frying.

Puree and serve with a few driblets of the paprika oil and a pinch of the jamon—but not too much, as it's salty and strong and will affect the flavor quickly.

Michael Gebert is a freelance food writer and the creator of skyfullofbacon.com, a Chicago-based video podcast and food blog.

## Every Day Is Soup Day

More than 30 years ago, Molly Fitzgibbon's grandma, frustrated by the difficulty of corralling her extended family for Thanksgiving and Christmas, invented her own family holiday: Soup Day.

Soup Day could be any old date—one year it was scheduled for the day of her hometown's Christmas parade; another year it celebrated an aunt's 90th birthday—but one day each year, when sons and daughters and aunts and uncles had no competing obligations, they'd all get together and eat soup.

Everyone would bring a soup—except Aunt Dollie, who provided hot ham-and-cheese sandwiches. The annual event is now a cherished family tradition, and one that Molly brought with her when she moved to Chicago from New Jersey.

An actor with a day job at the Chicago Park District, Fitzgibbon has found that her friends and colleagues have taken to Soup Day with a vengeance. One year she had 70 guests—and 18 different soups.

"It's just great to have this day that's just about getting together to eat and have a good time," says Molly. "Everyone should do it."

# MEMAW'S YEAST ROLLS
*from*
## CARA TILLMAN

Cara surprised us with these simple, flaky rolls made from her Grandma's recipe one night in 2010—and, well, we gobbled them up. They're best if served still warm. "They're based on a basic bread recipe that southern cooks have been making for many years," says Cara. "And they can be tweaked to suit different dietary needs and preferences." For vegan rolls, for example, swap out the butter and milk for vegetable oil and a bit more water .

### INGREDIENTS
MAKES 15 ROLLS

- 1 cup warm water
- 1 package yeast
- 3/4 teaspoon salt
- 1/4 cup sugar
- 1/4 cup milk
- 1 egg
- 1/4 melted butter, cooled (or vegetable oil)
- enough all-purpose flour to make dough stiff, about 5–6 cups

### PREPARATION

Mix yeast and sugar in a large bowl. Briefly work these two ingredients together with your fingers, as sugar helps activate yeast. Add warm water and stir. Let this mixture rest for about two minutes, until the liquid bubbles and foams slightly, an indication that the yeast is active. Add milk, butter (or other preferred fat), and egg. Stir. Incorporate 1 cup of sifted flour into the mixture and add salt. Continue adding flour until the mixture is stiff (3 to 4 cups). Cover with a towel and place dough in a warm, dry place to rise until doubled in size, about 1 hour.

Punch risen dough and knead for one minute, incorporating just enough extra flour to make sure the dough isn't too sticky to work with your hands. Pinch dough into 2–3 inch balls and place in a greased 9x13-inch baking pan. Allow rolls to rise until doubled again, about 1 hour. Bake in a 400°F oven for 11 minutes (or until golden).

Cara Tillman lives in Austin, Texas, where she's learning to be a teacher and working in a wine bar.

# CHEESE BREAD

*from*

## RAE HILL

This recipe comes from Chef Jeanne Kraus's breads class at the International Culinary School at the Illinois Institute of Art-Chicago, which, with Rae as liaison, donated their homework each week to Soup and Bread. Says Rae, "This is Chef Kraus's favorite recipe to teach and eat!" I can see why: These light, savory loaves, some of which were still warm, flew out of our bread baskets the week it was on the syllabus.

**INGREDIENTS**                    MAKES 1 FULL OR 2 SMALL ROUNDS

- 3 ½ cups bread flour
- ⅔ cups water
- 2 tablespoons olive oil
- 1 teaspoon salt
- 1 teaspoon instant yeast
- ¾ cup + 1 tablespoon levain
- ½ cup Parmesan cheese, ¼ grated, ¼ cubed

**PREPARATION**

Add all ingredients but cheese to the bowl of a standing mixer and mix on low for 3 minutes, adding water as necessary (dough will be a little stiff until cheese is added).

Mix another 3 minutes at medium speed to moderate gluten development.

Add cheese and mix until it is just incorporated.

Set aside in warm place to ferment until double in size.

Punch dough down and then shape into boules, then proof until doubled in size—or about an hour.

Place a pan of hot water on the lowest rack in your oven. Preheat oven to 425°F. Once you have placed the bread in the oven, quickly spritz the inside walls of the oven with water and shut the door fast to trap the steam. Bake 15–20 minutes. This creates the crisp crust on the bread. Then, lower temperature to 350°F to prevent overbrowning the cheese. Bake 20 to 30 minutes more, then cool at least 20 minutes before serving.

Rae Hill resides in Chicago, where she's living the dream with her husband Todd and working as a pastry chef.

# CHAPTER THREE

# Soup
## for MORE THAN
## Sustenance

*Five* o'clock on a chilly Tuesday evening and the line outside All Saints' Episcopal Church on Chicago's north side already stretches from the parish hall door half a block to the corner. Tuesday is food distribution day at Ravenswood Community Services, the nonprofit social service agency that runs—on the spindliest of shoestrings—a food pantry and community kitchen at the church.

Outside, the line will get longer: on an average Tuesday RCS serves a hot supper to 125 people and provides bags of milk, bread, and shelf-stable staples to at least 300. Inside, the Reverend Fran Holliday anxiously watches over the five hulking pots of veggies and stock she's got going at a rolling boil in the tiny basement kitchen.

Holliday's not usually the cook. RCS relies on regular rotating teams of volunteers to plan and prepare the weekly meal. And though you'd be tempted to call the RCS operation a "soup kitchen," soup is rarely on the menu. But the regular team, led by a local caterer, is on vacation, so Holliday has stepped in. She's never cooked for this many before, and she's going out on a bit of a limb with a hearty chicken noodle soup.

Soup's a challenge for RCS, she explains. Unlike a cafeteria-style operation, the Tuesday night meals are served family-style at large round tables—and it's a logistical challenge to deliver bowls of hot soup through the crowded parish hall efficiently. And those who come to RCS to cook and eat food—uniformly referred to as "neighbors"—often have specific nutritional needs that soup doesn't always meet. "We try to give people a lot of calories and protein," she says. "Something that will stick to the ribs."

She had stacks of canned chicken on hand, and she par-cooked 20 pounds of pasta shells on Monday. Now bowls heaped with chunks of chicken and pans loaded with pasta stand at the ready. "It's an experiment," she says, eyeing the bubbling pots. "We're just going to see how it goes."

"I really want to make sure we get a lot of gunk in there," says Jori, a medical researcher and experienced volunteer. She moves from pot to pot, ladling broth from each into a sixth pot to make room for the addition of plenty of protein and carbs.

Like most such efforts, the community kitchen and food pantry run on the backs of volunteers—some All Saints' parishioners, others neighborhood residents—30 to 50 of them every week. They cook and serve food, wash dishes, bag and distribute groceries, set up and break down chairs and tables, answer questions, and sit and talk with their neighbors during the meal.

"People come in and often they'll sit at the same table every week," says RCS executive director Wendy Vasquez. "They get here early so that they have time to get a cup of coffee and hang out. And we have a few volunteers who come, they sit at tables, and they just sort of get to know people and talk to people, and listen."

Free-associate on the word "soup," and "soup kitchen" may well be the first thing that comes to mind. Since the Middle Ages, Christian religious orders have offered free soup and bread to hungry petitioners, and the history of the United States is soaked in nondenominational soup. Some of the nation's earliest public-minded citizens—like James Ronaldson, who founded Philadelphia's Southwark Soup Society in 1804—took up ladles to serve free soup and bread to the "deserving poor." And of course the soup line is the classic image of the Great Depression, when millions of struggling Americans queued up for hot sustenance.

Today the need for a nourishing meal can seem almost as pressing. The Greater Chicago Food Depository—the huge food bank serving Cook County—counts 650 food pantries, soup kitchens, and shelters in its network of member agencies. Between them they serve an estimated 142,000 men, women, and children each week. The neighbors who come to Ravenswood Community Services for food each week are just a drop in the sea of the hungry nationwide, but it's clear that they're getting more than just a hot meal.

In the fall and winter of 2008, when the recession was hitting full force, the line out the door doubled in size. "People would be walking home from the train," says Vasquez, "and they'd come in and be like, 'What's going on? Do you need some help?' They would just literally jump off the street and volunteer."

Mike, an investment banker, landed in the kitchen for the first time by following just that trajectory: He was driving home from work, got curious about the line, and decided to get involved. Now there's an apron over his work clothes and he's tasked with slicing and apportioning pieces of pineapple-cherry-coconut "dump cake" into bowls for dessert while Fran and Jori distribute fistfuls of chicken and pasta among the pots, making sure they don't overflow, each stirring gently with a long wooden spoon.

"This almost looks like a pozole," says Jori, peering into a pot of what's now a dense, golden stew of shells, chicken, and veggies.

"Really, what we want is a 'stewp,' " says Holliday. "Somewhere between a soup and a stew."

By six the parish hall upstairs is full. Downstairs, Holliday nabs a few men

*Following are ten recipes for hearty,
protein-rich soups and stews starring
all manner of meats, from beef and
lamb to sausage and salt cod. Some
are trickier than others; all are
guaranteed to satisfy the gnawing
hunger of any carnivore—especially
when served with some hearty whole-
wheat sourdough bread.*

who'd been pondering a leaky pipe to begin hauling the pots of chicken soup up to a makeshift serving station. "Can I get all my volunteers in a line?" Jori calls out to the group, which by now includes a half-dozen more adults and several little kids, one of whom earnestly holds up his plastic-gloved paws for inspection.

"OK," says Jori. " We want to make sure we get the salad and the bread on every table first. Then, we have a soup station up there, where we're dishing the soup out into bowls on trays. You want to make sure every neighbor gets a big, hearty bowl of soup."

The volunteers grab bowls of bread and salad and head up to the dining room, where Holliday is wrapping up a blessing.

"Gracious God, we give you thanks for this community we have gathered here, and for this food we are about to share. Let us pray."

And then they're off—in a whirl of service and slurping. Wendy Vasquez joked later that she's always wanted to do a stop-motion film of a Tuesday-night meal. Once the doors open, she says, it's like a ball rolling down a hill—all you can do is stay out of the way. (I spent most of the meal pressed up against a wall, and accidentally flipped the light switch off twice. Oops!) Around me aproned servers—even the littlest ones—delivered the goods with surprising efficiency, leaning down to answer questions about the food and fielding requests for seconds.

"You did good, chef," says a server to Holliday, as she slips past.

The crowd is diverse: some older, some younger; some black, some white, some Asian. Some women, more men. The vast majority in attendance live within the 12 blocks surrounding the church. Eighty percent are elderly, members of the "working poor," or families living in the neighborhood. Twenty percent are homeless and living on the street.

In the northwest corner of the room, John and Jim sit with seven others at table 14—their regular spot. Jim—craggy face, gray hair and burly hands —has been coming to Tuesday dinners for six months or so. He heard about them through the American Indian Center down the street. I ask what he thinks of the soup.

It's good, he says—it's "Jewish penicillin," and then adds, "Me gusta la sopa!" He's studying Spanish.

John, on his right, is a lot younger. He's wearing a *South Park* T-shirt and has his hair combed back straight from his forehead. He used to work as a security guard for the CTA but was fired and has been out of work almost a year. His family's helping out so he can keep his apartment down the street while he looks for another security job, or something in retail. Or food service. Or, really, anything.

He discovered the Tuesday meals the same way Mike, the investment banker did: he saw the line.

"This is a great service to have for people who are down and out and need some assistance," he says, carefully. "It really does help them out. I have a place to live but some people here they're living in the road, or at a shelter. So every single Tuesday this is somewhere for them to go, something stable."

## Not Necessarily the New Normal

Hunger relief initiatives run the gamut: City agencies provide emergency food assistance to families in crisis; charities and churches regularly feed the poor. Planners track the location of grocery stores and strategize to eliminate so-called "food deserts;" community gardeners promote urban agriculture as a source of affordable, healthy food for all. But the key to eliminating hunger lies in addressing the roots of poverty, rather than chasing after it as it spreads.

As food activist Mark Winne, author of *Closing the Food Gap*, points out, there were no food banks in the United States in the 1970s; now, as the effects of Reagan-era cuts to the social safety net continue to ripple through an economy destabilized by recession, there are more than 200, serving more than 60,000 pantries and kitchens, and they provide our primary means of feeding hungry people. "That disturbs me," he says. "That we're perpetuating this system is problematic." He and others advocate for grassroots efforts to stamp out hunger, such as community cooking classes and workshops on smart shopping.

To help end hunger in your community you can volunteer at a pantry, teach kids how to cook, or look for a local food policy council to try and change the system—whatever suits your style. Online resources are plentiful—just get to Googling.

# BLACK-EYED PEA, CHORIZO, AND KALE SOUP
*from*
## TERRI GRIFFITH

I first met Terri back in the 80s, when we were both disaffected Pacific Northwest teens, and was thrilled when she turned up in Chicago. She based this soup on one she used to make as a cook at The Sisters restaurant in Everett, Washington. Usually, she says, "I'm a bean-soaking, stock-making kind of gal. But with 75 papers to grade this week, my usual from-scratch ethic did not happen. For Soup & Bread, I turned to a soup that can be hurried along by using canned ingredients. At The Sisters we made our own stock. I hope they don't think less of me." The lesson here? There's no shame in shortcuts.

## INGREDIENTS                    SERVES 14–16

- **12** cups (or 2 49-ounce cans) chicken stock
- **5** 15-ounce cans of black-eyed peas (well-rinsed)
- **1** large onion, chopped
- **1½–2** pounds chorizo
- **2** large bunches of curly kale
  olive oil

## PREPARATION

Bring chicken stock to boil in large pot and add black-eyed peas. Reduce heat. In a skillet, sauté onion in olive oil. Add to pot. In the onion skillet, cook the chorizo through, but not until dry. (When using chorizo in natural casing, you may press it out a little at a time into balls. It's not so important that they be round, but you're aiming for little bites of chorizo in your soup and not have it turn out crumbly like ground beef.)

Brown chorizo in batches. Do not crowd pan. Drain on paper towel and add to pot. Simmer on low for two hours stirring occasionally. A half-hour before you intend to serve your soup, skim any accumulated fat from the top. Chop kale into pieces and add to pot. Serve when kale is cooked yet still bright green.

Terri Griffith's novel *So Much Better* is published by Green Lantern Press. She loves soup.

# WHITE BEAN, KALE, KIELBASA, AND TORTELLINI SOUP

*from*

## ANASTASIA DAVIES HINCHSLIFF

Anastasia, a Hideout bartender and an all-around crafty lady, was one of our very first Soup & Bread cooks. She brought this beans-and-greens concoction (adapted from an *Epicurious* recipe) for our inaugural soup night in 2009, and brought her two young sons for family dinner almost every Wednesday for three years running.

**INGREDIENTS**                SERVES 8

- 1 pound dried white beans such as Great Northern, cannellini, or navy
- 2 onions, coarsely chopped
- 2 tablespoons olive oil
- 4 garlic cloves, finely chopped
- 5 cups chicken broth
- 8 cups water
- 1 (3 x 2-inch) piece of Parmesan rind
- 2 teaspoons salt
- 1 bay leaf
- 1 teaspoon finely chopped fresh rosemary
- 1 pound smoked kielbasa (fully cooked), sliced crosswise into ¼-inch pieces
- 8 carrots, halved lengthwise and cut into ½-inch pieces
- 1 pound kale, stems and center ribs discarded, leaves coarsely chopped
- ½–1 pound cheese tortellini (fresh or boxed)
  salt and pepper

**PREPARATION**

Cover beans under 2 inches of water in a pot and bring to a boil. Remove from heat and let stand uncovered 1 hour. Drain beans and rinse. Set aside.

Cook onions in oil in an 8-quart pot over moderately low heat, stirring occasionally, until softened, 4 to 5 minutes. Add garlic and cook, stirring frequently, for 1 minute. Add beans, broth, 1 quart of water, cheese rind, salt, pepper, bay leaf, and rosemary and simmer uncovered until beans are just tender, about 50 minutes.

Stir carrots into soup and simmer 5 minutes. Stir in kale, sausage, tortellini, and remaining quart of water and simmer, uncovered, stirring occasionally, until kale is tender and pasta is cooked. Season with salt and pepper to taste.

Anastasia Davies Hinchsliff is a mother, gardener, bread maker, and soup eater. She lives in Chicago.

# ESCAROLE AND WHITE BEAN SOUP WITH TURKEY-PARMESAN MEATBALLS

*from*

## CELESTE DOLAN

Proving that whole "great minds" thing, Celeste also brought a beans-and-greens based soup for the 2009 debut of Soup & Bread. Which was great because the only thing better than one hearty soup is two at the same winter table. Where Anastasia relied on kielbasa for a meaty kick, Celeste went with delicately flavored turkey meatballs.

**INGREDIENTS**                    SERVES 8

BEANS

- ¾ cup cannellini beans
- 10 cups water
- 5 sage leaves
- 3 cloves garlic, peeled and left whole
- 2 bay leaves
- 3 tablespoons olive oil
- 1 teaspoon salt

MEATBALLS

- 1 egg
- 2 tablespoons water
- ¼ cup bread crumbs
- 12 ounces ground turkey
- ¼ cup grated Parmesan
- 2 tablespoons flat leaf parsley, finely chopped
- 2 garlic cloves, minced
- ¾ teaspoon salt
- ¼ teaspoon pepper
- 6 tablespoons olive oil

SOUP

- ½ pound escarole
- 1½ cups carrots, cut into ¼-inch dice
- 1 tablespoon olive oil
- 8 cups homemade chicken stock or canned low-sodium chicken broth
  salt and pepper

## PREPARATION

BEANS: Pick through beans to remove stray grit. Place in large bowl and cover with water. Soak overnight. Next day, in large pot, combine beans, 10 cups water, sage, garlic, bay leaves, and oil. Bring to a boil and add salt. Reduce heat to bring beans to a simmer. Simmer for about 1 hour or until beans are tender, but not mushy. Strain beans, discard garlic, sage, and bay leaves. Set beans aside.

MEATBALLS: In medium-sized bowl whisk together egg and water. Mix in bread crumbs until just moist. Add ground turkey, Parmesan, parsley, garlic, 3 table-spoons olive oil, salt, and pepper. Stir until ingredients are combined. With wet hands, shape turkey mixture into ¾-inch diameter meatballs. Place on a cookie sheet or some such and chill 30 minutes.

In large frying pan, heat 1½ tablespoons olive oil over moderate heat. Add half the meatballs to pan and cook, making sure all sides are browned, about 2–3 minutes. Remove the meatballs from pan and drain on paper towels. Repeat with remaining oil and meatballs.

SOUP: Trim ends of escarole. Separate leaves and wash thoroughly. Cut crosswise in 1-inch strips. In stockpot over moderate heat add oil and carrots. Sauté until carrots are almost tender. Add the escarole, 1 teaspoon salt, and stock. Bring to a simmer over moderate heat, stirring occasionally. Add meatballs and bring back to a simmer. (Meatballs should be done once broth comes back to a simmer.) Add beans and return to simmer. Adjust seasoning with salt and pepper. Serve warm with Parmesan shavings.

Celeste Dolan founded her catering company after working for two decades as a graphic designer. Her keen design sense informs Celestial Kitchens, where she prepares a marvelous array of baked goods and savory goodies.

# DELI-STYLE SWEET AND SOUR SOUP WITH SHREDDED FLANK STEAK

*from*

## ROGER GREENE

When Roger, a professional personal chef, served this soup on April 1, 2009, someone said it was so good it tasted "like cabbage candy." Patience is key to developing the sweetness—make sure to let the soup bubble along at a very low simmer for at least an hour.

### INGREDIENTS

SERVES 8

- ¼ cup vegetable oil
- 1 large yellow onion, coarsely chopped
- 1 clove garlic, minced
- 1 pound flank steak, well trimmed of fat
  salt and fresh-ground pepper to taste
  lemon pepper, to taste
- 1 teaspoon caraway seeds
- 8 cups beef broth
- 1 pound tomatoes, canned with juice
- 1 8-ounce can tomato sauce
- ⅓ cup fresh lemon juice
- ¼ cup dark brown sugar
- ¼ cup golden raisins
- 1 head Savoy or green cabbage, cored and cut into ½-inch shreds
- 2 bay leaves
- 4 teaspoons fresh parsley, chopped
- 2 tablespoons fresh dill, chopped
  sour cream or yogurt (optional)

### PREPARATION

In a large pot, warm oil over low to medium heat. Add onion and garlic and sauté 2–3 minutes or until translucent. Lightly season the flank steak with salt and pepper, add to pan, and sauté 2–3 minutes on each side, turning once, until lightly browned.

Add beef broth and deglaze the pan by stirring and scraping to dislodge any browned bits. Add diced tomatoes and tomato sauce. Then add lemon juice, sugar, raisins, cabbage, lemon pepper, caraway seeds, and bay leaves. Raise the heat and bring to a boil. Reduce heat to low, cover partially and simmer gently until the meat is tender, about 1 hour.

# Filling Up With Empty Bowls

Launched in 1990 by Michigan art teacher John Hartom, the international program Empty Bowls holds fundraisers at churches, schools, community centers, field houses, and art galleries—with pottery as the come-on. Ceramists donate handmade bowls, which are sold, rinsed, and then used on the spot as the vehicle for a simple meal of soup and bread. At the end of the night guests go home with the bowls and the funds go to a local food bank, soup kitchen, or other hunger-relief organization.

The proceeds from the annual Empty Bowls nights held at Chicago's Lillstreet Art Center benefit an independent organization founded by Chicago chef Mary Ellen Diaz, who gave up a successful career in fine dining to fight hunger firsthand. Her nonprofit, First Slice, provides home-cooked restaurant-quality meals every week to about 100 homeless or impoverished men, women, and children.

First Slice also trains cooks—many of them formerly homeless or living in poverty—who provide the vats of soup that fuel the event.

In 2010 Empty Bowls drew more than 350 guests and raised $12,000. Attendees fussed over the multitude of bowls on offer while helpers filled soup warmers and ferried baskets of bread into the service area. As the line for soup grew, children arrived at their tables clutching bowls brimming with corn chowder and potato-leek. They crowed over their prizes and compared notes on their favorites. By 9 PM the bowl room was almost empty; only a few lumpy efforts remained.

Chicago and its suburbs are home to at least seven annual Empty Bowls events, and hundreds more are staged around the world each year, from Finland to Australia. If you want to start your own, you can order an info packet that includes basic principles and helpful hints for $5 at emptybowls.net.

Discard bay leaves. Remove the meat from the pot and, using a sharp knife and fork, cut and tear it into coarse, bite-sized shreds. Stir meat back into soup; add chopped parsley and dill. Taste and adjust seasoning if necessary. Ladle into bowls and top with a dollop of sour cream or yogurt if desired.

Roger Greene is a Johnson & Wales University-trained personal chef who has been happily cooking for clients in the Chicago area for over seven years.

# CARBONNADE FLAMANDE
*from*
## NIALL MUNNELLY

Carbonnade flamande is the Flemish equivalent of beef bourguignon, a hearty farmer's food that has found a place in gastropubs and on Slow Foodists' tables for its emphasis on a few simple, high-quality ingredients. It's also, says Niall, "what I promised to prepare before I realized I hadn't a prayer of making the two to three gallons requested for Soup & Bread, so I did what any resourceful chef would do: I whinged until my girlfriend offered to make some stock and scared up some useful vegetables to add a little volume to the dish. This recipe is for a traditional carbonade, prepared in a Dutch oven."

**INGREDIENTS**                 SERVES 6

- **3** pounds lean beef, cubed
- **3** medium white onions, finely chopped
- **1½** cups of Flemish sour ale (Rodenbach, Monk's Cafe, or the like. Belgian brown ales, like Chimay, Ommegang, etc. are also good. Big bottles are good; you'll have the rest to drink with the meal.)
- **2** strips of thick, chopped-up bacon
- **1** teaspoon butter
- **2** bay leaves
- a pinch or two of thyme
- **2** teaspoons mustard
- **½** teaspoon parsley
- **1** teaspoon currant jelly or a fruity lambic (cassis or framboise work well) for a little tart sweetness at the end
- sea salt and coarsely ground black pepper

**PREPARATION**

Preheat your oven to 350°F. I sweat the bacon in the oven as it preheats, removing the pieces when much of their fat has rendered and they're still fairly soft. Leave the pieces on a paper towel and reserve half a teaspoon of the grease. Generously season the beef with salt and pepper and brown the cubes with a dash of olive oil, transferring them to the Dutch oven when done.

I've learned over several attempts that browning with flour doesn't add much more to the stew than an alkaline flavor that needs to be compensated for later, and that the careless chef who uses too much oil serves the guests a greasy, deeply unpleasant meal. Since you're not making a roast, all that fat has nowhere else to go. Trim your meat assiduously, and use as little oil as possible—and then use less than that. Get the meat as dark as you can stand, and your patience will be rewarded in the end. Add the pieces of bacon to the meat and, lowering the burner to medium-low, brown the onions in the teaspoon of butter and reserved bacon grease. You want these onions to be richly caramelized and soft, as dark as you've made the meat, so cook slowly and be sure to stir the onions occasionally; they should be a uniform brown, but not burnt.

Transfer the finished onions to the pot, and deglaze the pan with the ale over high heat, using your spatula to scrape all that goodness from the bottom of the pan. When the beer is boiling and foamy, pour it into the pot, and add bay leaves and thyme. Cover the Dutch oven and place it in the oven for at least two hours, stirring only occasionally. Three's better, and four better still, but you have to find your own sweet spot between immediate gratification and melt-in-your-mouth meat. Five minutes before serving, stir in the parsley, mustard, and jelly or lambic. A little squeeze of lemon heightens the flavors and adds clarity, but it's easy to overdo.

I like to eat carbonade with whipped or coarsely mashed potatoes and garlic, or with roasted root vegetables, and usually pair it with the same beers I used for the recipe. But you can eat your stew with that double IPA in your fridge or a red Bordeaux, if you prefer; it's a forgiving meal. For extra credit, toast some leftover stew with a sharp, crumbly cheddar cheese over tortilla chips for Nachos Belgium. I'm not kidding. Don't forget the Sriracha sauce.

Niall Munnelly is another aspiring musician with a desk job, but he's always wanted to work in a record store, tend bar, and fight crime. He's constantly looking for ways to add more beer to his diet.

# MINT CREEK FARM'S
# IRISH-STYLE SHEEP STEW

*from*

## DANIELLE MARVIT

It took a while to reheat this rich stew at Soup & Bread, and as it slowly warmed it unleashed a heady aroma of rosemary and lamb. Frankly, the wait was agonizing, but ultimately worth it. The stew tasted as good as it smelled, if not better. When Danielle brought the stew to the Hideout she was working for Mint Creek Farm, which raises grass-fed sheep on the alfalfa and clover of east-central Illinois; she has since moved back home to Western Pennsylvania with her husband and is busy feeding folks organic fruits and vegetables grown at Churchview Farm.

**INGREDIENTS**                    SERVES 12

- **1** pound mutton stew meat (from either shoulder or neck)
- **1** pound lamb stew meat (from either shoulder or neck)
  kosher salt and cracked black pepper (to taste)
  olive oil
- **2** cups homemade broth (preferably lamb, but beef works too)
- **1** 12-ounce bottle of Goose Island Oatmeal Stout
- **1** yellow onion, sliced
- **2** carrots, unpeeled and sliced on a diagonal
- **4** cloves garlic, smashed and sliced
- **1** pound baby potatoes, any color (Danielle used yellow)
- **1** celery stalk, sliced on a diagonal
  paprika, to taste
- **½** oz of fresh rosemary, finely chopped

**PREPARATION**

Day One: Season mutton and lamb with salt and pepper. (May brown meat in pan, but not necessary). Add both meats to a 3-quart Crock-Pot. Drizzle a little olive oil (or use the same pan the meat was browned in and use the fat that renders off the meat) in a sauté pan and add the sliced onion. Season the onion with salt, pepper, and paprika. Cook until translucent, then add the garlic and cook a little longer until garlic is fragrant. Add the onion and garlic to the Crock-Pot. Add a little more olive oil to the pan then add the carrots, celery, and potatoes. Toss the vegetables to coat, season with more paprika (and salt and pepper, if needed) and then add them to the pot. Pour the oatmeal stout into the sauté pan and cook until the alcohol fumes are no longer present. Stir to make sure that all the seasoning and browned bits from the pan are iincorporated into the warmed beer. Add the beer and the broth to the Crock-Pot; turn it on to low and cook for 8–10 hours, or until the meat is so tender it falls apart. Cool to room temperature and then refrigerate overnight.

Day Two: Skim off any cooled fat that accumulates on the surface of the pot. Reheat the stew in the Crock-Pot. Gently stir in the fresh rosemary and serve with additional oatmeal stout and crusty bread. Enjoy!

Danielle Marvit loves mutton chops and mopeds.

# HAM HOCK AND HABANERO SOUP
# WITH CORNMEAL-PLANTAIN DUMPLINGS

*from*

## MEGAN LARMER

Megan brought this complex, Jamaican-inspired stew to Soup & Bread on a March day when the forecast called for icy rain. The day before, she says, she'd found herself staring into her freezer for inspiration. Staring back was a ham hock bought from the back of a local farmer's van and a bag of habaneros she'd grown in the summer, so she began dreaming of a place these ingredients would be at home together. As it turned out, this was a great dish for a cold day. While reminiscent of the tropics, it definitely stuck to your ribs. After a bumpy bus ride to the Hideout, the dumplings hadn't held their shape quite as planned, but cooking them right in the soup resulted in a thickened broth that gave the soup some nice weight.

## INGREDIENTS                    SERVES 10

### SOUP

- **8** cups smoked pork stock (recipe on page 196)
- **1** ham hock (reserved from making stock)
- **1** pound carrots, peeled and chopped
- **1** bunch green onions, white part minced and green part chopped
- **4** cloves garlic, minced
- **3** limes, zest two of them
- **2–3** inches of fresh ginger, minced
- **1–4** habaneros (depending on spiciness), minced
- **2** tablespoons ground allspice
- **1** teaspoon ground cumin
- **2** teaspoons ground thyme
- salt
- vinegar

### DUMPLINGS

- **2** cups cornmeal
- **2** eggs
- **2** ripe plantains (black peels), diced
- **¼** cup flour
- **½** teaspoon cinnamon
- **½** teaspoon nutmeg
- **1** tablespoon sugar

## PREPARATION

SOUP: Warm stock in a large pot over low heat while you render the fat from the trimmings of the ham hock you used to make your stock (page 196) in another pot over low heat. When the bits of ham are good and crispy and you've got a good little oil slick in there, remove the bits of hock. Then add carrots, garlic, ginger, lime zest, the white part of the green onions, habaneros, and the dry spices with a dash of salt. Let that all sweat together over low to medium heat until the carrots are tender but not mushy. Pull the meat off of the ham hock, throwing out cartilage and such, and add that to the mix. Pour your hot stock into the pot. If this doesn't look like enough soup to you, round it out with some chicken stock or boiling water, or beer, or whatever. Bring to a high simmer.

DUMPLINGS: Mix the cornmeal with enough boiling water to make a very stiff dough. While that sits, dice the plantains. Add the flour, spices, sugar, and a dash of salt to the cornmeal. Break the eggs in a bowl and mix them up with a little water. Stir the eggs into the cornmeal. If the dough looks too loose, add more flour or dry cornmeal; too stiff, add water. It should look like a dense cornbread batter. Stir the plantains into the dough.

Finish it up: Squeeze the limes' juice into the soup. Taste your broth and correct the seasonings (it probably needs salt), then bring it to a high boil. Drop the dough by teaspoonfuls into the broth. You may need to let a batch cook, then drop more in to keep them from sticking together. When all the dumplings are cooked (you can tell because they will float), turn off the heat. Taste the broth again, add a dash of vinegar if you like. Throw in the chopped green parts of the onion. Eat!

Megan Larmer is on the board of Slow Food Chicago, training to be a Master Gardener through the University of Illinois Extension, and working as part of the Chicago Rarities Orchard Project to establish an urban community orchard dedicated to rare fruit varieties. She was honored to be chosen as a delegate to Slow Food International's Terra Madre Convivium in 2010.

# HAM HOCK, TORTELLINI, AND BEAN SOUP

*from*

## DUNCAN BAYNE

My father made and served soup to homeless Seattleites out of the kitchen at the Episcopal cathedral in that city for many years, so this project has, unsurprisingly, tickled his soup bone. He contributed this recipe for a hearty, oh-so-hammy almost-stew, and I prepared it to his specs for Soup & Bread 2010. He suggests noshing on some of the boiled ham with crackers as you cook. If you eat too much, you can dice up a small ham steak and add it to the soup, for extra meat. But, he says, stick to the hock if you can: "The flavor differential is ginormous."

## INGREDIENTS

SERVES 10–12

- **3–4** pounds smoked ham hock (or knuckle, or whatever else it's called in your neck of the woods)
- **16** cups of water
- **1** Mayan sweet onion (or Walla Walla, or Vidalia), roughly chopped
- **¾** cup celery, chopped
- **2** large carrots, chopped
- **1** 15-ounce can of cannellini beans (drained)
- **1** 15-ounce can of black beans (drained)
- **1** package tortellini, any flavor
- **1** cup chopped cabbage (optional)

## PREPARATION

In a large pot, cover ham hocks with water and let slowly boil for at least 3 hours. The meat will fall off the bone and the stock will emit a luxurious aroma. You should end up with something like 10 cups of stock (having started with 16 cups of water).

Let the stock congeal overnight, then remove bones and defat it before you use it. In a separate pan, sauté onion, celery, and carrots. After 10 minutes or so toss the sauté into the soup stock and add beans.

Let simmer for a while (how long is probably not important, but at least until the beans are cooked through), then toss in a package of tortellini. (We used one that had a sweet Italian sausage filling, but one could just as well use a cheese filling.) Add a handful of chopped cabbage, if you've got it. Let it all cook for a few minutes more, then chow down.

Duncan Bayne is a father of three gorgeous but demented girls, husband of gorgeous wife (mother of the three), lawyer, trustee for foster children, cook, active Episcopalian, and soon to be fully retired.

# CALDO VERDE
*from*
## CHRISTOPHER SULLIVAN

This Portuguese soup can accommodate just about any type of sausage. For us Christopher used linguica, a full-bodied tube steak exuding the clean flavors of pork, garlic, and paprika. But, he says, smoked kielbasa or even a supermarket brand will suffice. Same for the broth. Chicken is standard, but he prefers to use a vegetable stock (see page 189). Feel free to spice to taste.

## INGREDIENTS                    SERVES 12

- **3** tablespoons of olive oil
- **1** large yellow onion, diced
- **3** cloves garlic, thinly sliced
- **1** pound pork sausage, (kielbasa, chorizo, linguica)
- **2** bunches kale, cleaned and torn into small pieces, discard heavier bits of stems
- **3** baking potatoes, peeled quartered
- **10** cups stock or water
- **1** tablespoon kosher salt
  fresh ground black pepper
- **2** tablespoons Sriracha chili sauce

## PREPARATION

Heat the olive oil in a large Dutch oven or stockpot over medium heat. Add the onion, and sauté until translucent but not browned, stirring frequently, about five minutes or so. Slice the sausage into ¼-inch coins, and add to the oil and onion and sauté, continuing to stir frequently. You want the sausage to release its oils and flavors into the pan a bit. Add the garlic and sauté for three more minutes, stirring constantly.

When fragrant, and when the sausage has started to caramelize a bit, add the broth and bring to a light boil. Add the potato and all the kale, cover, and simmer for about 30 minutes until the kale really begins to soften. When the potato is tender enough, mash pieces with the back of a spoon to break up until all the potato is either bite size or creaming into the soup. Season with the salt and pepper, and add the Sriracha to taste. I like to add a little at a time and let it cook for a bit longer and taste again, since the soup will continue to develop spice.

Serve with a crusty piece of bread, or a crostini, a little drizzle of olive oil, and hot sauce on the side. Enjoy!

Christopher Sullivan is the chef at Ikram, a restaurant and boutique in downtown Chicago. He previously worked at Blackbird for many years.

# SALT COD AND CHORIZO CHOWDER

*from*

## ANDREA LEE AND TIM FISTER

This soup seems plain and rustic on its face, but is utterly surprising—not too fishy, very savory. And that generous pinch of saffron—the most expensive spice on the planet—gives it a sophisticated exclusivity. Known as "bacalaou" in Portugal, "klip-pfisk" in Norway, and "marue seche" in France, salt cod is just that: cod that's been preserved by salting and drying. Layered over a creamy potato base and cast against the spicy sausage it is, among other amazing properties, not even all that salty.

**INGREDIENTS**                         SERVES 12

- **2** pounds salt cod, even thickness if possible
- **2–4** tablespoons butter (depending on healthy vs. yummy preference)
- **2** heads garlic, fine dice (about ½ cup)
- **3** pounds Yukon gold potatoes, coarse dice
- **2** large yellow onions, diced
- **12** cups chicken stock, low sodium
  generous pinch saffron
- **½** pound cured (Spanish-style) chorizo, fine dice
- **4–6** Fresno peppers, fine dice (or similar lightly spicy pepper)
  salt and pepper to taste
- **2** cups whole milk
  two handfuls parsley, chopped
  zest from one lemon

## PREPARATION

Soak salt cod in water or milk for 2 days, replacing the liquid every 12 hours or so. Before you start cooking, drain liquid.

Sweat onions in butter and add garlic after a few minutes in a big pot. Add potatoes, chicken stock, and saffron; bring everything to a simmer.

Meanwhile, in a separate pan, sauté chorizo until it releases much of its oil. Add peppers to the pan for a minute, and then remove from heat and pat sausage down with paper towels.

When potatoes are fork tender, add the drained cod. When the cod is cooked through, break it up with your spoon. Add the cooked chorizo and peppers to the mix. Add milk, and season with salt and pepper to taste. Turn off heat and add parsley and lemon zest.

It might sound hard, but it's really not! And if you think a different way might taste better, you're probably right, so you should try it.

Andrea Lee tries to help local Ys around the country better serve their communities during the day and is crazy lucky to come home each night to her husband, Tim Fister. Somehow, Tim cooks up yumminess daily after spending his days at Argonne National Lab looking at tiny particles doing tinier things that might just save the world by making energy storage more efficient.

# WHOLE WHEAT SOURDOUGH
## MADE FROM RYE STARTER

*from*

### CHRIS SCHOEN

Chris adapted the recipe for this dense, hearty bread from Andrew Whitley's *Bread Matters*. The advantage to this method, he says, is that that if you already have rye starter on hand, you can have a loaf ready in as little as 9–10 hours. (If you don't have any rye starter on hand, give yourself an extra 4–5 days to get it ready.) Once made, rye starter can live undisturbed in the fridge for up to a month without needing refreshment.

**INGREDIENTS**          MAKES ONE ROUND LOAF

RYE STARTER
- rye flour
- water

PRODUCTION STARTER
- ⅔ cup rye starter
- 1½ cups + 2 tablespoons whole wheat flour (for a lighter loaf substitute up to 1¼ cups white flour)
- ½ cup water

DOUGH
- 3⅓ cups whole wheat flour (or mix of whole wheat and white)
- 1¼ cups water
- 1¼ teaspoons salt

## PREPARATION

RYE STARTER: Mix 3 tablespoons plus 1 teaspoon rye flour with ¼ cup water. Seal in an airtight container and set aside for 24 hours. On the second day, add the same amount again of flour, and water. Mix, seal, and set aside for 24 hours. Repeat on the third and fourth days. As soon as the second day the starter should start to become bubbly and aromatic. By the fourth day, you will have 1¼ cups of active starter—more than you need for this recipe. Keep the rest in the fridge for your next loaf. If it needs to be augmented, continue to add flour and water in the increments above (keeping the starter at room temperature during this period) until you have the amount you want.

PRODUCTION STARTER: Mix all into a firm dough, cover, and set aside for 3–4 hours.

DOUGH: Combine flour and water and knead until the gluten begins to develop, then add the production starter and salt. Continue to knead until the gluten is fully developed (dough should be elastic) then cover with plastic wrap or a flour-dusted kitchen towel for one hour while the dough rests. Then, shape dough into a ball, and proof in a bowl or proofing basket, seam-side up, covered with a flour-dusted towel, for another 3–5 hours, until loaf is aerated.

Thirty minutes or so before baking, preheat the oven to its hottest temperature, placing a Dutch oven or casserole on the middle rack.* Carefully invert the loaf seam-side down onto a baking peel or cookie sheet which has been dusted with cornmeal, flour, or wheat bran. Slash the top with a razor three or four times at roughly a 45 degree angle. (This keeps the top from bursting in the oven). Then slide the loaf into the Dutch oven, reduce the oven temperature to 425°F and bake covered for 30 minutes. After 30 minutes remove the top of the Dutch oven and bake for another 20–25 minutes, until done. Let bread cool completely before slicing.

*If you don't have a suitable casserole or Dutch oven, this bread can also be baked on a cookie sheet or pizza stone.

Chris Schoen, who lives in sunny, clement Chicago, is a member of Theater Oobleck's artistic ensemble. He is currently working on a series of cantastoria based on Charles Baudelaire's *Les Fleurs du Mal*.

# CHAPTER FOUR

# Chili for Competition

The day the Chicago Bears lost the 2011 NFC championship to the Green Bay Packers, a very different battle was building over on Chicago's west side, between the brick walls of the Empty Bottle rock club. A diminutive man rocking a Freedom Isn't Free T-shirt and a stars-and-stripes bandanna kicked things off, bellowing—as he hopped around the floor in front of a stage piled high with electronic equipment: "Are you ready for some CHILI!?! Woooo! America! Football!! Goddamn chili!!!! And, ahh...synthesizers!"

It was the first ever Synth Chili Cook-off. Beardy boys and pale girls, their faces obscured by windshields of horn-rimmed glasses, gazed at the stage intently, nodding as one young man coaxed blippy electronic noise and fuzzy loops of feedback from the gadgetry onstage. What it all had to do with the dark complex of spices underpinning his Aztec Secret chili was anyone's guess. But it really didn't matter. Chili cook-offs? They're everywhere, thrown by and for just about everybody.

Sure, there's your standard VFW hall competition. Your church throwdown. And of course, your Super Bowl party. But once you start looking you'll see chili fans in ever-more unlikely places. I found chili cook-offs everywhere from a gay dance club to an indie printshop. At a studio for developmentally disabled artists, supporters competed under such noms de stockpot as "Team Quacktastic" while an MC raffled off aprons and art by program participants. At a sprawling microbrewery jam-packed with firefighters dressed for duty, the chili was judged by a bank of food writers under the glare of TV lights, to a soundtrack of blaring classic rock.

What is it about chili? How has this savory combo of slow-cooked meat and fiery peppers secured a cultural niche unrivaled by any other stovetop dish? Why is macho culinary prowess proved through chili rather than, say, chicken noodle soup?

"Chili just goes better with beer," said a cook at Spudnik Press, a small printmaking studio hosting a chili competition to raise money for its move to larger digs. (Victors in both meat and veggie categories took home a gold-painted squeegee as their prize.)

"It's such a core American thing," said a contestant at Sidetrack, a cavernous dance club in Chicago's Boystown whose chili contest shared a day with cook-offs thrown by a crew of Yelpers on the south side and a group of fringe theater artists to the far north. "We're a melting pot, but every region has its own culture and its own recipe—so there's a little ego and a little pride all mixed in."

Plus, said a young volunteer at the same event, "It's just one of those things that traditionally masculine guys can make. Even if they don't cook, they'll grill and barbecue and make chili—and get really into it."

Titus Ruscitti, a part-time bartender and freelance writer who blogs under the name "Chi BBQ King," is the three-time winner of an annual chili contest thrown by *Time Out Chicago* magazine. He pegs chili's competitive nature to its possible cowboy roots. "Maybe back in the day it was a way to get together that was better than having a gunfight?"

History is murky on the origins of this most American of stews. Titus pointed me toward *Chili Madness*, by Texas Chili Society founder Jane Butel, who says chili may have developed as road food for Texan prospectors in search of California gold—a mix of dried beef, fat, and peppers meant to be rehydrated on the lonesome trail. Unless it really evolved in Texas prisons in the mid 19th century. Or began as cowboy chow cooked up over a campfire. Or, as legend has it, was introduced to the New World by a Spanish missionary channeling the visions of a beautiful teenaged nun. Seriously.

But while chili's origins may be uncertain, the location of the world's first chili cook-off is generally agreed upon. It was held in 1952 at the Texas State Fair in Dallas by author Joe E. Cooper to promote his new chili cookbook, *With or Without Beans*. The event drew 55 contestants but failed to settle the question posed by the book's title—and the prospect of chili made with beans was enshrined as blasphemous to any self-respecting Texan. But 15 years later a Texas journalist named Frank Tolbert—promoting his own history of chili, *A Bowl of Red*—put cook-offs on the map for good.

Tolbert's contest, held in the Rio Grande town of Terlingua, Texas, pitted Homer "Wick" Fowler, head cook of the Chili Appreciation Society International, against a New York writer named H. Allen Smith, infamous in Texas chili circles for a humorous magazine piece titled "Nobody Knows More About Chili Than I Do." Smith's chili recipe called for beans. The fight was on.

That contest also ended in a tie—and the beans/no beans debate continues to this day (see page 81). But the Terlingua championship now draws thousands of chili enthusiasts to that remote Texas town every year, and around the country CASI (chili.org) sponsors hundreds of cook-offs, which raise an estimated $1 million a year for the ALS Assocation and other charities.

And that's the thing: Chili cooks may get into it for the glory, but cook-offs themselves usually serve the greater good.

The Arts of Life is an art studio for developmentally disabled adults located in a low-slung industrial building on Chicago's west side. The program held its second annual chili cook-off fundraiser in November 2010, in partnership with the local microbrewery Half Acre. When I wandered in, late in the evening, the brick warehouse was wall-to-wall with artists and supporters quaffing Daisy Cutter Pale Ale and queuing up for chili and artisanal gelato.

"We're an art studio that actively engages people both with and without disabilities," Tim Sarrantonio, the group's outreach coordinator, told me as he dished up Dixie cups of his venison-and-turkey-based Red Dawn Rising Chili. "So right there it's all about community." With the cook-off, he pointed out, "You can have upwards of 100 people in one space enjoying the same basic thing, but then they've all got their own individual flair." And, as executive director Denny Fisher told me later, it's great for the studio's artists—many of whom live in residential programs—to see food as something fun and social.

Or, as a cook at the Spudnik Press cook-off put it, chili cook-offs can be a mirror of your community—in his case, Chicago's independent art scene: Every artist may have his or her own style, but there's plenty of work to go around. "Everyone's got their own niche—much like chili. This is just a friendly way to get the competition together."

*The nine recipes that follow all offer something to thrill—or infuriate—the most die-hard chili enthusiast. Beans? Check. Venison? Yup. Vegetarian? You got it. Serve them up with a side of soothing buttermilk-corn muffins for a quintessential meal.*

# CHILI
*from*
## TOM V. RAY

This recipe is adapted from Jay Pennington's chili, which won the International Chili Society's coveted title of World Champion Chili way back in 1977 and has been widely circulated ever since. This is chili for the Texas purists out there. In other words: No Beans.

## INGREDIENTS                    SERVES 16

- 1 tablespoon vegetable oil
- 3 medium onions, finely chopped
- 2 bell peppers, finely chopped
- 2 celery stalks, finely chopped
- 6 garlic cloves, finely chopped
- 8 pounds coarse ground round steak
- 2 20-ounce cans tomato sauce
- 2 20-ounce cans stewed tomatoes
- 1 6-ounce can tomato paste
  water, as needed to achieve desired consistency
- 1 4-ounce can chile salsa
- 1 3-inch green canned hot pepper, finely chopped
- 6 ounces chili powder
- 1 4-ounce can green diced chile
  dash of oregano
  salt to taste (approximately 3 tablespoons)
  pepper to taste (coarse ground)
  garlic salt to taste

## PREPARATION

Put oil in a 10–12 quart pot over medium heat. Add onion, bell pepper, celery, and garlic. Cook until onion is transparent. Add meat gradually, stirring till browned.

Add the remaining ingredients, stirring to incorporate thoroughly after each addition. Lower heat and simmer for 2 ½ to 3 hours. Stir frequently to prevent scorching.

Tom V. Ray grew up on a farm in southwestern Indiana and now lives in Chicago. He has been playing bass professionally since 1983.

# BEEF CHILI
## WITH RUSTIC DUMPLING NOODLES
*from*

### JOSH HUDSON

Chili over spaghetti is a classic Cincinnati dish, but I'd never heard of putting noodles *in* the chili until Josh brought this savory pot adapted from his mother's family recipe. For a lighter version, substitute ground turkey for the beef.

**INGREDIENTS**  SERVES 12

CHILI

- **3** pounds ground beef
- **1** medium-large yellow onion, chopped
- **1** teaspoon minced or crushed garlic
- **1** 7-ounce can chipotle peppers in adobo sauce
- **1** 28-ounce can diced tomatoes
- **1** 5-ounce can tomato paste
- **1** 28-ounce can black beans
- **1** teaspoon adobo sauce (from can)
- **1** pint dark beer
- **4** heaping tablespoons chili powder
- **1** heaping tablespoon ground cumin
- **1** heaping tablespoon ground coriander
- **1** heaping tablespoon cocoa powder
- **1** heaping teaspoon ground ancho chiles
- **1** heaping teaspoon instant coffee
- **½** teaspoon cinnamon
- **1** cup water

NOODLES

- **1½** cups all-purpose flour
- **½** teaspoon salt
- **2** eggs

**PREPARATION**

CHILI: Brown ground beef with onion and garlic. (If a large sauté pan is not available, this may be done in two batches.) Drain most of the fat and add the beef to a large soup pot. Add 2 chipotles, minced, and 1 teaspoon adobo sauce; set can aside. Add remaining non-noodle ingredients and water. Simmer for about 40 minutes, stirring regularly so the bottom does not burn.

When done simmering, taste for seasoning; add salt and more chili powder if desired.

NOODLES: While chili is simmering, make noodle dough. Combine flour and salt in mixing bowl. Add eggs and, using a fork, fold them into the dry ingredients until

# Beans or No Beans, the Proof Is in the Powder

Every pot of chili is a reflection not just of the pride (and prejudices) of a cook—it's also statement about place. New Mexico's chili verde relies on pork, tomatillos, and ample amounts of the state's signature green chiles. Cincinnati chili comes spiked with sweet notes of cinnamon and cloves and is served, notoriously, over a plate of spaghetti. And Texans hold up the iconic "bowl of red" as chili stripped to its essentials: Slow-cooked beef, chile pods and chili powder. Garlic, some onion. And maybe—just maybe—tomatoes. But never, ever beans.

This prohibition is so strong that no bean-bearing chili is allowed to sully the competition at Terlingua—birthplace of the anthem "If You Know Beans About Chili, You Know That Chili Has No Beans."

What's the matter with beans? History is as vague on this as it is on the origins of chili itself—and most of the answers seem to come down to "because." But one plausible explanation is that beans can provide cover for less than ideal chili powders. Just as no soup can rise above a pallid stock, so the heartiest chili can't overcome old, stale spice.

As Titus Ruscitti said, "If you use, like, McCormick powder off the grocery shelf that's just not gonna do it."

Titus and many others recommend making your own chili powder. Recipes abound online, but, basically, you want to toast equal parts ancho chiles (dried poblanos) and New Mexico chiles, along with a few chiles de arbol or cayenne peppers. For something smokier, use chipotles as well. Something fruitier? Try guajillos. Whatever you've got, cut them all in half and bake them on a cookie sheet until they're lightly crispy, then pulverize them to a powder in a blender or food processor. Mix in some toasted cumin seeds, maybe some garlic powder, maybe some Mexican oregano. And voila! Fresh, potent seasoning that will give your chili a fearsome backbone—with or without beans.

---

just combined. If mixture is too gummy, add flour; if too dry and crumbly, add teaspoons of water until mixture coheres.

Flour hands. Drop teaspoon-sized lumps of noodle mixture into chili until mixture is gone. Simmer 20 minutes, continuing to stir. If soupier texture is desired, add more water. Serve with grated cheese if desired.

Josh Hudson plays rock music with Grimble Grumble, the Thin Man, the Titmice, and the Hildegard Knef.

# SAUSAGE CHILI
*from*
## DOUG SOHN

Doug—owner of Hot Doug's, Chicago's storied hot dog stand showcasing all manner of exotic tube steaks—was a ridiculously helpful Soup & Bread cook. Once his giant pot of chili was gone he stuck around to bus tables and wash dishes and just generally display the charm and good sportsmanship for which he's become famous. But dragging this recipe out of him was no picnic! All he would give up for months was: "Make chili. Add 40 different kinds of sausage." Eventually we wheedled the secret out of him. Quantities are a little vague, but that's the way chili rolls. Be careful with those hot peppers: a little goes a long way.

**INGREDIENTS**                    SERVES 16–20

- **2** pounds beef brisket
  olive oil
- **2** yellow onions
- **2** green bell peppers
  hot peppers to your heat level (jalapenos, Anaheim, banana, finger hots, poblanos, whatever)
- **4** cloves garlic
- **1** 28-ounce can chopped tomatoes
- **1** 28-ounce can whole peeled tomatoes
- **1** 28-ounce can crushed tomatoes
- **1** 5-ounce can tomato paste
- **3** 14-ounce cans beans (black, kidney, cannellini, Great Northern, whatever)
  cumin, chili powder, black pepper, Tabasco, garlic powder, onion powder, celery salt, coriander to taste
  cooked sausage, as much and as many kinds as you like (the more the better!)

## PREPARATION

Heat a large stockpot on medium-high, add some olive oil and sauté the chopped beef brisket until browned. Remove from stockpot and set aside.

Add some more olive oil. Sauté diced onions and diced bell peppers until soft. Remove from stockpot and set aside.

Add some more olive oil. Sauté chopped hot peppers until lightly browned. Add a lot of chopped garlic and continue cooking until the garlic starts to lightly brown.

Deglaze the stockpot with beer—Doug prefers Rolling Rock but any brand will work. Drink the rest of the beer if there's any left.

Add cans of chopped tomatoes, whole peeled tomatoes (crush by hand after they've simmered a bit), crushed tomatoes, and some tomato paste to the stockpot, and then return the brisket and the onion/pepper mixture back into the pot as well.

Add drained cans of beans (black beans, kidney beans, cannellini beans, Great Northern beans, whatever) to the stockpot.

Season with cumin, chili powder, and black pepper.

Simmer for an hour or so. Make sure it's not too dry. Add tomato sauce and/or more beer if needed.

Check seasoning. Add, to taste, any or all of the following: Tabasco, salt, more cumin, more chili powder, garlic powder, onion powder—did I mention more cumin?—celery salt, coriander.

Add sliced cooked sausage. The more varieties the better.

Serve topped with shredded sharp cheddar cheese and a dollop of sour cream.

Note: This chili is better if allowed to cool and refrigerated overnight, then reheated the next day.

Doug Sohn is the owner of Hot Doug's, the Sausage Superstore and Encased Meat Emporium in Chicago.

# VENISON CHILI
*from*
## ROB MILLER

Rob used venison "harvested" by his father in northern Michigan. It is, he points out, a very lean (and free-range) meat, with a mild flavor. "Your fears of it being too gamey will go unfounded," he says, reiterating that chili, by its very nature, is improvisatory. "Cooking times vary. It can be as little as an hour, or as long as six in a Crock-Pot. It's done when it's done, you know?" If you've got some peppers lying around, throw them in, he says. Chili's "casual that way."

**INGREDIENTS**                    SERVES 8

- **1** pound ground venison
- **1** 16-ounce can of crushed tomatoes
- **1**  cup finely chopped cilantro
- **1** can of corn
- **1-2** cayenne peppers, chopped fine (Remember, wash your hands—and no eye rubbing!)
- **3-4** cloves of garlic, minced
- **½** can light lager (Here's a chance to put that Schlitz to good use.)
- **1** 15-ounce can each: dark red kidney beans, chili beans, Great Northern beans (Yes, I use canned beans.)
- **3** tablespoons chili powder
- **2** tablespoons salt
- **1** tablespoon paprika
- **1** tablespoon cumin
- **2** tablespoons sugar
- **3** tablespoons bacon drippings
-  couple dashes of Worcestershire sauce, soy sauce, and Tabasco.
- **½** tablespoon cornstarch (optional)

## PREPARATION

Brown the venison over low heat with the garlic, cayenne peppers, half the spices, and all the dashes. Since it's so lean, you'll need to use some sort of cooking oil. I use 2 tablespoons of the bacon drippings.

While this is browning, find a stew pot and empty in the beans, the delicious bean juice, corn, cilantro, the other half of the spices, the half can of beer, the remaining bacon drippings, and half a cup of water and set over medium heat. Let that simmer for 30 minutes. Cook may now finish other half of beer.

Add the venison and the tomatoes. Adjust the seasoning and let it simmer happily away till dinnertime. If it's too watery, mix the cornstarch with another half cup of cold water and stir into the pot slowly, then let it cook down to the desired consistency.

I like to serve it with some very sharp cheddar cheese grated on top and some crusty bread on the side.

Rob Miller is the co-owner, co-founder, and chief executive bon vivant of Bloodshot Records, and harbors a perhaps-unfortunate bias against soups that are meant to be served cold.

# CEDAR VALLEY SUSTAINABLE FARM BEEF AND PORK CHILI

*from*

## BETH AND JODY OSMUND

Beth and Jody have been valiant Soup & Bread supporters, driving in every winter from their farm in Ottowa, Illinois, adorable kids in tow, to serve up an annual soup. This phenomenally hearty chili showcases their sustainably raised beef and pork.

### INGREDIENTS                    SERVES 12

- ½ cup vegetable oil
- 1 pound ground beef
- 1 pound ground pork
- 2 large onions, chopped
- 6 cloves garlic, sliced (or 4 teaspoons minced garlic)
- 2 tablespoons chili powder
- 1 tablespoon cayenne pepper
- 1 tablespoon ground black pepper
- 1 tablespoon kosher salt
- 1 tablespoon fresh lime juice
- 2 12-ounce bottles dark beer
- 1 24-ounce can tomato sauce
- 3 14-ounce cans diced tomatoes
- 46 fluid ounces (5¾ cups) tomato juice
- 3 14-ounce cans chili beans
- 1-2 large, dried ancho peppers

### PREPARATION

Heat oil in a large stock pot over medium heat. Crumble the beef and pork into the pot, and cook, stirring frequently, until the meat is no longer pink. Add onion, garlic, and spices and cook until onions soften.

Add the lime juice and beer. Stir in the tomatoes, tomato sauce, tomato juice, and beans. Drop in dried peppers and simmer for several hours. Taste periodically and add spice as desired. (Jody sometimes adds a tablespoon of cocoa power for a rich, smoky taste.)

Serve with bowls of chopped scallions, sour cream, cilantro, and grated cheddar.

Jody and Beth Osmund run Cedar Valley Sustainable Farm, home to Illinois' first community-supported meat-sharing subscription. The Osmunds raise beef, chicken, and pork along the banks of Indian Creek in rural Ottawa. At CVSF it's all about the food: raising it, cooking it, and eating it!

# LAMB AND BLACK BEAN CHILI

*from*

## ANDREA NEWBERRY

Andrea always hated chili as a kid. That is, until her mom went on a diet and in her attempts to make healthy meals came across a low-fat recipe of stewed lamb and black beans in red wine and chili powder. The result of mom's reducing efforts is this lean, tangy chili, so different, in Andrea's memory, from the "thick, gooey, beany" stuff she hated.

### INGREDIENTS       SERVES 8

- 1½ pounds ground lamb
- 1 medium onion chopped
- 2 garlic cloves, minced
- 1 28-ounce can whole tomatoes, drained and chopped
- 1 cup dry red wine
- 1 tablespoon chili powder
- 1½ teaspoon ground cumin
- 1½ teaspoon dried oregano
- 1 teaspoon sugar
- 3 15-ounce cans black beans, drained
- salt to taste
- hot sauce to taste

### PREPARATION

In cooking pot, sauté lamb, onion, and garlic. Add tomatoes, red wine, and seasonings up to and including sugar, and bring to a boil. Allow to simmer for 2 hours. Add black beans and simmer for 30 more minutes.

Season with salt and hot sauce to taste. Garnish with cilantro and fresh jalapenos.

You can find Andrea Newberry at forkableblog.com.

# BISON AND SQUASH CHILI

*from*

## LAWRENCE PETERS

Bison, or American buffalo, were at risk of extinction 100 years ago, but thanks to aggressive conservation efforts the mighty beast has made a big comeback—so much so that it's now an excellent, sustainable source of red meat. It's always free range and raised without antibiotics or growth hormones, and cooks like Lawrence prefer it for its lean and strong, clean flavor.

### INGREDIENTS                    SERVES 12

- ½ cup chopped red onion
- 3-5 cloves garlic, crushed
- 1 tablespoon olive oil
- 1 pound ground bison meat (or lean ground beef)
  ground black pepper
- 2 tablespooons chili powder
- 1 teaspoon ancho chili powder
- 1 teaspoon powdered chipotle pepper
- 1 tablespoon rubbed sage
- 3 bay leaves
- 1 cube vegetable bouillon
- 3 cups uncooked butternut squash, peeled and cubed
- 3½ cups cooked black beans
- 3½ cups cooked white kidney beans
- 2 28-ounce cans fire-roasted tomatoes, with juice, chopped
- 1 12-ounce beer (I used a medium-bodied ale, but use whatever sounds good)
  water (as needed)
  salt

**PREPARATION**

In a large pot, sauté the onion and garlic in olive oil. When slightly translucent add bison, and a healthy amount of black pepper. Add chili powder, ancho, and chipotle pepper, and cook meat until brown.

Add all other ingredients, and simmer until squash is tender—about 3 hours. Salt to taste.

Note: The chili should be thick and savory but not dense, and it should have a little kick to it. I usually serve this over some chopped rapini cooked al dente in a little chicken stock, and top the bowl with a squeeze of lime.

Lawrence Peters is a country singer, songwriter, DJ, and drummer. When not tending bar at the Hideout he can be found performing with a variety of bands or spinning all manner of records on almost any night of the week.

# THE EX'S VEGGIE CHILI
*from*
## SARAH KAVAGE

Sarah supplied a vat of this spicy vegetarian chili to our 2011 Soup & Bread in Seattle. She hit up a neighbor for the recipe and gives her all due credit—or more specifically, she credits her neighbor's marital difficulties. "She got it from her ex-husband, who owned a restaurant back in the day," Sarah says. "In my recollection, this is the only nice thing my neighbor has ever said about her ex, so I figured it must be good."

**INGREDIENTS**                    SERVES 25

CHILI

- 2 tablespoons olive oil
- 1 small red onion
- 1 small yellow onion
- 4 teaspoons chopped garlic
- 3 teaspoons chili powder (I used chipotle)
- 2 teaspoons chili flakes or 1 fresh hot pepper, minced
- 2 tablespoons cumin
- 1 zucchini, celery stalk, or carrot
- 1½ cups garbanzo beans
- 3 cups black beans
- 4 cups kidney beans
- 2 bottles Guinness
- 1 tablespoon Greek oregano
- 2 20-oz cans tomatoes
- 1 red pepper
- 1 green pepper
- 10 cloves
  dash of liquid smoke
  salt and pepper
- 4 large bay leaves

CILANTRO SOUR CREAM

- 16 ounces plain yogurt
- 8 ounces sour cream
  half a bunch chopped cilantro
  salt
  juice from 1 lime and 1 orange

**PREPARATION**

CHILI: Sauté the onions, celery, and garlic in the olive oil, adding the cumin and oregano halfway through. Then add this mix to the beans, along with the tomatoes, the Guinness, and the chili powder and/or chile. Simmer half an hour; then add the rest of the veggies. Simmer slow and low until ready to serve.

CILANTRO SOUR CREAM: The recipe called for goat cheese and cilantro as a garnish; for Soup & Bread I made a cilantro sour cream: mix together all ingredients listed, and then top each bowl of chili with a little dollop.

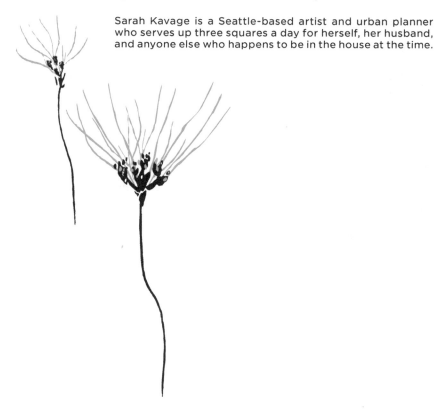

Sarah Kavage is a Seattle-based artist and urban planner who serves up three squares a day for herself, her husband, and anyone else who happens to be in the house at the time.

# WHITE BEAN CHICKEN CHILI
*from*
## RAVENSWOOD COMMUNITY SERVICES

The kitchen at Ravenswood Community Services dishes up a free supper for more than 100 every week in conjunction with the organization's food pantry (see page 52). The focus at RCS is on providing a high-protein meal that'll stick to the ribs, and this dense chicken chili sure fits the bill. Hot pepper freaks may find it to be on the mild side, but as with all chili, feel free to adjust to taste.

### INGREDIENTS                    SERVES 20

- **4** cooked chicken breasts, chopped
- **2** 15-ounce cans great Northern beans, drained
- **¾** cup chopped onion
- **1** red pepper, chopped
- **2** jalapeno peppers, diced
- **2** cloves garlic, minced
- **2** teaspoons ground cumin
- **½** teaspoon salt
- **1** teaspoon dried crushed oregano
- **4** cups chicken broth or stock
  - sour cream
  - tortilla chips
  - Monterey Jack cheese, grated

### PREPARATION

Combine all and slow cook in Crock-Pot for 8–10 hours on low or 4–5 hours on high.

Top with garnish of choice. Enjoy!

Volunteers at Ravenswood Community Services prepare and serve a hot family-style meal to hungry neighbors every Tuesday night in the parish hall at All Saints' Episcopal Church at 1757 W. Wilson in Chicago.

# BUTTERMILK-CORN MUFFINS
*from*
## ALLISON STOUT

Per Allison this recipe is adapted from one for buttermilk-cheddar cornbread in the December 2002 issue of *Bon Appetit*. The muffins make a terrific soothing counterpart to any seriously spicy chili.

**INGREDIENTS**                    MAKES ABOUT 12 STANDARD MUFFINS

- **1** cup flour
- **1** cup yellow cornmeal
- **⅓** cup sugar
- **2** teaspoons baking powder
- **1** teaspoon baking soda
- **1** teaspoon salt
- **4-6** ounces grated sharp cheddar cheese
- **1** cup frozen corn kernels (or fresh, if in season)
- **1** tablespoon olive oil
- **1** tablespoon butter
- **1** cup buttermilk
- **½** cup heavy cream
- **2** eggs
- **¼** cup melted butter, cooled

**PREPARATION**

Preheat oven to 400°F. Use butter or baking spray to grease a 12-cup muffin tin. Heat 1 tablespoon olive oil and 1 tablespoon butter in a skillet over medium-high heat. Add corn to skillet. Stirring frequently, cook corn for 3–4 minutes or until heated through and fragrant. Remove from heat and let cool.

Whisk first 6 ingredients in large bowl to blend. Mix in cheese. In a separate bowl, whisk buttermilk, cream, eggs, and melted butter to blend. Add buttermilk mixture and cooled corn (along with any fat from pan) to dry ingredients and stir just until incorporated, taking care not to overmix. Let batter rest for 5 minutes, then spoon into prepared muffin tin, filling each cup about ¾ full. Bake about 18–20 minutes, or until muffins are golden on top.

Devour.

Allison Stout is in charge of savory pies at Hoosier Mama Pie Company and provides catering, cooking instruction, and personal chef services under the name Seriously Good Food.

# CHAPTER FIVE

# Soup for Art

"**Oh** my god—how cool would it be if we let people pick where they want to sit and put the tables together themselves? They'd be self-directing their experience!" That's Amy.

"Yes! It's like, 'We've already envisioned the beginning for you—now we're giving the tools to make it yourself!'" That's Kate.

It was Super Bowl Sunday and the snow was falling fast, but in the loft above the Mexicantown Bakery, on the southwest side of Detroit, neither the weather nor Vince Lombardi were on anyone's mind. Instead, Kate Daughdrill and Amy Kaherl were pondering decorating logistics. The space was littered with chairs, dusty tables, throw pillows, garlands of shredded newspaper, and mysterious pieces of wood, and in less than three hours more than 100 people were expected for soup.

More precisely, they were coming for Detroit SOUP, a monthly dinner started by Kate and musician Jessica Hernandez, whose parents own the bakery building, as a way of bringing together friends, fellow artists, and community organizers to talk, make connections, and raise a little bit of money for worthy projects. Guests pay $5 for soup, salad, and bread, and at some point in the night various creative types stand up and pitch their current projects—and explain how they could use a couple hundred bucks. Eventually the diners step into a custom-built voting booth to cast ballots, and the project with the most votes takes home the door. In 2010 Detroit SOUP raised about $4,500, in increments of $300 or $400 at a time. Its beneficiaries included an initiative to manufacture thermal "sleeping bag" coats built by and for the city's homeless and a hand-drawn, limited-edition Detroit coloring book.

One year later, SOUP was at a turning point. The first event drew maybe 20 people. Now enthusiastic crowds showed up the first Sunday of every month, and organizing had become a full-time unpaid job. After this one, Kate and Jessica were planning to scale back to quarterly meals and Kate, an MFA student at nearby Cranbrook Academy of Art, would be stepping away to focus on her own artwork. Amy, a seminary student turned grant administrator, would be taking the reins.

"Every time I do SOUP," she said, "It feels sort of like what ministry is supposed to be. I mean, you're bringing people together and creating community around something beautiful, and asking really good questions. What could be better than that?"

People in Detroit talk like this a lot: Forging strong new communities in their embattled city is in the forefront of many minds. But Detroit SOUP is just one of (at last count) 27 such artist-driven soup projects around the world.

Chicago artists Bryce Dwyer and Abby Satinsky credit their friend and co-collaborator Ben Schaafsma with seeding the idea, basing it on a soup subscription service in his hometown of Grand Rapids. When Ben moved from Grand Rapids to Chicago to go to art school, he joined up with Abby and another student, Roman Petruniak, to start the arts collective InCUBATE; Bryce joined them a year later. In 2007 they launched a program called Sunday Soup in their storefront space next to Chicago's historic Congress Theatre.

Sunday Soup happened once a week for about a year—a casual get-together that raised perhaps $125 to $250 a week for local, small-scale art projects. But as people who've thrown themselves into a labor of love will tell you, they're a lot of work.

"We wanted to create an immediate and simple source of funding for creative projects," Abby reflected in a 2010 essay for the Chicago-based *Proximity* magazine. "Yet this project is also dependent on the volunteer labor of the organizers.... What is our responsibility to keep the thing going, even though it can sometimes feel like another full-time job? Is it really sustainable if it depends on us in this way?"

In 2008, InCUBATE swapped the weekly events for a monthly Sunday Soup brunch and joined in a collaboration with the collective Material Exchange to install a week long soup café in New York City's Park Avenue Armory, as part of "Democracy in America," a project of the arts organization Creative Time. In a space outfitted with repurposed and scavenged furnishings, they invited a handful of artists and fellow travelers to cook soups and give talks. The cafe raised $1,500 to fund a large-scale installation by artist Robert Snowden, but its impact rippled far beyond that one project, as artists and administrators who'd been at the show toted the model home with them. InCUBATE also held Sunday Soups in Houston and Buffalo, and Creative Time published a "Democracy in America" book, featuring Sunday Soup, and soon similar food-based fundraisers were popping up all over the map.

"By going to these exhibitions we met a lot of people," says Bryce, "and the book circulated widely, and it sort of instantly made legitimate this weird meal thing we did in Chicago."

From Seattle to Dubuque to Kiev these initiatives vary wildly in scope and structure—and they're not limited to soup: Brooklyn FEAST (Funding Emerging Art with Sustainable Tactics) serves meals for 2,000 out of a Greenpoint church basement. Baltimore Stew is a collaboration between an artists' collective and an anarchist bookstore, serving four-course meals cooked from locally sourced produce and raising money for social justice projects. Philly Stake (get it?) is funded by a grant from the Pew Foundation; the Hartford FEAST was founded by a city councilman.

As interest in cooking and alternative food systems grew, the mainstream media took note. In August 2010, Detroit SOUP was profiled in the *New York Times*; in April of the same year Saint Louis's "Sloup" turned up on the NPR program "Marketplace."

Ben Schaafsma didn't get to see his idea take off—he died a month after the Armory show, in October 2008, after he was struck by a car in New York City. In the wake of his death, InCUBATE retrenched, and reassessed. In late 2010 they launched sundaysoup.org, which serves as a clearinghouse for information about similar food-based fundraisers nationwide, but Chicago's Sunday Soup is on hiatus.

*In homage to the open-source, fluid nature of Sunday Soup, Detroit SOUP, and the myriad other arts-based soup projects around the globe, this chapter reflects the progression of an idea. Here you'll find six variations on a theme— specifically, the theme of tomato soup, as it evolves from essential tomato-basil to an inspired concoction called "pizza soup" by its creators. These soups are paired with a recipe for the ciabatta that is a mainstay of Soup & Bread— with a fun twist on the basic loaf provided as well.*

"On an emotional level," says Abby, "this was something Ben worked really hard on, and to see it make its way out in the world is really meaningful in a really, really deep way. I don't think any of us have any interest in being proprietary. Something really great has started, and what's important is that I feel a meaningful connection to people in different places that I would never have had the opportunity to have."

Up in the Motor City SOUP was transforming the loft above the bakery. Under the direction of an artist friend, strings of tiny white lights had been hung around the bar and draped over tents on the stage. "Trees" topped with newspaper pom-poms anchored piles of pillows, creating what Amy dubbed "pods of community" around café tables stacked with crates of thrift-store dishes. A dozen doors donated by a local architectural salvage firm leaned against one wall, waiting to be turned into long, low tables by the diners, per the afternoon brainstorm.

And then the crowd tromped in from the snow. Cute 20-somethings in retro-80s fashions mingled with coverall-clad artists and a handful of well-turned-out types in pumps and pencil skirts, waiting for that night's soup—a veggie, tomato-based "stone soup," complete with rock in the bottom of the pot. But first Kate gave a little speech, and brought seven of the 2010 grant recipients up to the mike to give quick updates on their projects.

"I was running on empty," said Veronika Scott, the College of Creative Studies student who founded the Empowerment Plan, the "sleeping bag coat" project. She was broke, burned out, and about to give up when she won a SOUP grant last year. The money gave her the fuel to pitch her plan to Carhartt, which signed on to fabricate 25 initial coats. In January she was on CNN.

During the meal other diners got up to talk about the soup projects they were starting at home: In Hamtramck, in Dearborn, and at an apartment complex in Detroit called Spalding Court.

"We just want to give this idea away," said Kate from the mike. "Just as we were inspired by other soup projects to do our own, we want you to feel free to take the idea home with you and do what you want with it. Because the real work always gets done in small groups, in our neighborhoods and our communities."

# CREAMY TOMATO SOUP WITH BASIL
*from*
## JESSICA AND TARA LANE

This soup pops with the unadulterated essence of fresh summer tomatoes—and when it was served at Soup & Bread the tomatoes weren't even fresh. They'd been harvested at the Hull-House farm and canned at the peak of tomato season, part of food preservationist Tara Lane's program to educate the public about seasonality. For more about Hull-House, soup, and food see page 114.

**INGREDIENTS**                    SERVES 10

- ¼ cup butter
- ¼ cup olive oil
- 1½ cups chopped onions
- 3 pounds tomatoes (cored, peeled, and quartered or preserved canned tomatoes)
- ½ cup chopped fresh basil leaves
- salt to taste
- ground black pepper to taste
- 4 cups vegetable broth
- 1 cup heavy cream
- sprigs fresh basil for garnish

**PREPARATION**

Heat the butter and olive oil in a large pot over medium heat. Stir in onions and cook until tender. Mix in tomatoes and chopped basil. Season with salt and pepper. Pour in the chicken broth, reduce heat to low, and continue cooking 15 minutes.

Blend soup until smooth. Return to pot (if necessary) and bring to a boil. Reduce heat to low, and gradually mix in the heavy cream. Pour soup through a strainer before serving. Garnish each serving with fresh basil.

Jessica Lane is a chef at the Jane Addams Hull-House Museum at the University of Illinois at Chicago. She studied at Le Cordon Bleu of Western Culinary in Portland, Oregon, and graduated from the School of the Art Institute of Chicago in 2007. There she studied various forms of design, from painting to textiles, which she cites as a constant influence on her work as a chef.

Tara Lane is a chef, an activist, and the food preservationist at the Jane Addams Hull-House Museum. She acted as one of the first programming directors for Common Threads and has consulted on product development for Starbucks, Quaker Foods, and Naked Brands. She launched her own product line, Sweet Girl Desserts, in 2008.

# WHITE BEAN, TOMATO, AND BASIL SOUP
*from*
## MONICA AND LAURA FOX

Laura, the official Soup & Bread recipe wrangler, was invaluable to this project—and after spending months staring at others' soup recipes she decided to stir the pot a bit with her own contribution. She and her mom, Monica, each made two gallons of soup—Laura in her apartment in Chicago's Wicker Park, and Monica in her home on the far south side. They learned something in the process: Even with the same recipe, soups naturally reflect their makers. While Monica's pot was light and chock full of basil, Laura's was creamier, the result of extra starchy potatoes.

## INGREDIENTS                            SERVES 12

- **4** 15-ounce cans of cannelini (white) beans
- **1** tablespoon olive oil
- **1** large onion, finely chopped
- **4** cloves garlic, minced
- **10** cups low-sodium chicken broth
- **1** bouquet garni: 1 bay leaf, 1 sprig parsley, 1 sprig fresh thyme (wrap these into a coffee filter with a rubber band or twist tie around it)
- **1** tablespoon tomato paste
- **½** teaspoon dried thyme
- **½** pound new potatoes, peeled and diced
- **1** 16-ounce can diced tomatoes with liquid (don't drain!)
- **2** medium zucchini sliced, or a bunch of green beans or spinach
- **3** tablespoons fresh basil, chopped

## PREPARATION

Sweat the onion and half the garlic in the olive oil until translucent. Add the white beans, water, chicken broth, bouquet garni, and diced potatoes and simmer for one hour.

Add remaining garlic, tomatoes, tomato paste, and thyme and simmer for 20 minutes. Stir in vegetable and a dash of pepper and simmer for 15 minutes.

Stir in fresh basil and you're done.

Monica Fox is a master cook who has delighted her family, friends, neighbors, and acquaintances with her culinary creations since she was nine years old.

Laura Fox is happy to call herself Monica's daughter, and shamelessly plunders whatever recipes she can from her mother.

# TOMATO-FENNEL BISQUE
## WITH PARMESAN TUILES
*from*
### THE HEARTY BOYS

The Hearty Boys shot to fame as winners of the first season of the Food Network's reality competition *The Next Food Network Star*. In 2005 they launched their own TV show, in 2007 they published their own cookbook, and in 2011 they made soup for Soup & Bread! Only, not this soup. There was a tomato-sized hole in our recipe collection, so while Dan and Steve delivered a very tasty yam-chipotle puree to the actual event, they graciously contributed the specs for this delicate, elegant bisque to the book. I tried it at home and the fragrant fennel triangulates wonderfully with the tomatoes and cream.

### INGREDIENTS                    SERVES 6

SOUP

- **1** medium fennel bulb, thinly sliced (about 2 cups)
- **1** shallot, thinly sliced (about 2 tablespoons)
- **4** tablespoons olive oil
- **1½** cups vegetable stock
- **½** cup white wine
- **1** 28-ounce can good-quality tomato puree
- **1** tablespoon kosher salt
- **½** teaspoon ground white pepper
- **½** teaspoon ground fennel seed
- **2** tablespoons honey
- **2** cups heavy cream
- **1** tablespoon fennel seeds, for garnish

PARMESAN TUILES

- **1** cup shredded Parmesan cheese

## PREPARATION

SOUP: Put a small skillet over high heat and add the fennel seeds. Dry toast them in the pan, shaking often, until they begin to color a medium brown. Remove from the pan and set aside.

Pour the oil into a large saucepan and add the fennel and shallot. Place over medium heat and cook, stirring occasionally, until the fennel begins to wilt, about 10 minutes. Add the wine and vegetable stock and bring to a boil. Reduce the heat and let simmer another 10 minutes, until the fennel is soft. Add the tomato puree, salt, pepper, ground fennel, and honey and let simmer another 15 minutes. Remove pan from heat and blend soup until smooth. Return to the saucepan (if necessary) and stir in the cream. Put the pan back on medium heat and let come to a simmer. Add more salt and pepper to taste.

PARMESAN TUILES: Line a baking sheet with parchment paper and spray lightly with cooking spray. Form small piles of cheese 3 inches in diameter. Place the pan in a 350°F oven and bake until golden brown throughout. Remove from the oven, let cool 2 minutes, and then peel each circle from the paper and roll into a cigar shape. Let cool and store in a cool dry place. Garnish each bowl of soup with one tuile.

Dan Smith and Steve McDonagh, aka the Hearty Boys, won the first season of *The Next Food Network Star* and went on to host *Party Line with the Hearty Boys*. They have appeared on CBS's *The Early Show* and have been featured in the *New Yorker*, the *New York Times*, and other publications. They live in Chicago, where they operate their catering business and the restaurant Hearty.

# SPICY TOMATO AND BACON SOUP

*from*

## JENNIFER BERMAN

Jennifer was part of a crew drawn from the ranks of LTH Forum, a Chicago-based culinary chat site, who participated in Soup & Bread for two years running. We were thrilled to partake of the collective soup savvy of this group of food freaks, and sorry we couldn't include every one of their recipes. It was a tough choice, but this one was a real standout: deceptively simple and addictively good.

**INGREDIENTS**                    SERVES 6–8

- **6** slices of thick-cut bacon
- **2** 28-ounce cans of San Marzano tomatoes
- **1** cup carrot, small dice
- **1** cup onion, small dice
- **½** cup celery, small dice
- **½** cup garlic, minced
- **¼** cup olive oil
- **1** teaspoon thyme
- **1** teaspoon red chili flakes (increase or reduce to taste)
- **1** tablespoon sugar
  salt and ground pepper to taste
- **1** tablespoon dried basil
- **3** cups chicken stock
- **1** cup 2% milk
- **½** cup light sour cream or low-fat Greek yogurt
  fresh basil chiffonade

- **1** cup sourdough bread cubes
- **2** tablespoons olive oil
- **1** tablespoon minced garlic
  salt and pepper

## PREPARATION

Fry the bacon until crispy, set aside to drain. Reserve bacon fat. Chop bacon (small dice). Gently squeeze the juice out of the canned tomatoes (reserve juice and set aside), spread tomatoes on a baking sheet, drizzle with olive oil, salt, and ground pepper and roast in 450°F oven 10–15 minutes until dried.

In large pan, sauté onions in bacon fat and 2 tablespoons olive oil; after about 3 minutes, add garlic. After another 2 minutes, add carrot and celery and sauté until all vegetables soften (add more oil if too dry).

In stock pot, heat remaining olive oil if needed (depends on how dry the veggies are at this point) and add previously cooked vegetable mix, dried tomatoes, thyme, chili flakes, sugar, and dried basil, cooking and stirring until all are incorporated. Add reserved tomato juice and chicken stock (2 cups at first, may add more to desired consistency and flavor) and bring to a simmer.

Once heated through, puree until smooth. For larger batches of soup, a standing blender may be required to get the soup to the right consistency—or you can just go with a slightly chunkier soup.

Add milk and sour cream and continuing pureeing. Add all but 2 tablespoons of the bacon (for crispier texture, you may want to crisp up the bacon again briefly before adding into the soup) and bring up to a full simmer again; cook for 10 minutes, give or take. Taste, add additional salt and pepper as needed.

To make garlic croutons: sauté bread cubes with olive oil and garlic until lightly crispy. Add salt and pepper, let cool, and store covered in a dry place.

Garnish soup with croutons, a sprinkle of bacon, and basil.

Jennifer Berman is a happily non-practicing attorney who guides companies in managing their human resources needs. She avidly indulges her two passions—culinary arts (both cooking and eating) and canine rescue. And no, the dogs don't get to sample (much).

# PAPPA AL POMODORO
## (Tuscan Bread Soup)
*from*
### GABE McMACKIN

Catering chef Gabe McMackin brought a huge pot of this traditional Tuscan peasant fare to the Brooklyn installment of Soup & Bread in 2010. It is ridiculously good—rustic and simple and full of sunny flavor. It's also eminently adaptable. "It's a great platform if you want to put other things in it like mussels," says Gabe. "It's great if you just want to eat it by itself. It's great with a chunk of smoked pork or a prosciutto rind in there, and it's great vegan."

## INGREDIENTS                    SERVES 6-8

- **4** cups peeled San Marzano tomatoes lightly crushed by hand, cores removed
- **1** loaf ciabatta, crusts peeled off (at least bottom crust), torn into 2-inch chunks, very, very stale, or dried well in a low oven
- **4** cloves garlic, sliced
- **1** teaspoon fennel seed
- **1** teaspoon chili flakes
- **1** jalapeno or serrano pepper
- **4-8** cups vegetable stock (or more, to taste)
- **2/3** cups best quality extra virgin olive oil
  salt and pepper
  Reggiano Parmesan—a chunk for grating and then the rind for the soup
  basil

## PREPARATION

Heat a large pot over medium heat. Add the olive oil, then the garlic, and cook until it gets fragrant and starts to color, about 20 seconds. Add the fennel seed, chili, and jalapeno and cook for a few seconds more.

Add the tomatoes, salt and pepper, basil, and Parm rind if you're using one and bring to a boil. Knock the heat back to a simmer, and let it cook for a half hour or so to pull out some of the acid. Stir.

Add your bread—and it better be S.T.A.L.E. It picks up better flavor, and if it's not stale it reverts to big knots of raw dough that are tough and gnarly and gross. Let the bread soak up some tomato, then start adding your stock. It'll need a lot. And it'll keep needing more. Start with a few quarts, maybe 3, then see what happens. Reseason. Stir. A lot. The bread will burn on the bottom if you're not careful and your soup will be bitter and the children will cry and it'll be terrible. So stir. Bring it up to a simmer, let the bread get really hydrated, and let the flavors gush around with each other. Add more stock if you want.

## Soup as Art: Bill Drummond's Soup Line

Would you let a strange man into your house? You might if he were Bill Drummond—and if he came to make soup. Best known as the prankster who, as half of the British avant-pop duo the KLF, once set fire to £1 million in bank notes, Drummond is a conceptual artist wrangling with the concept of commodification. In 2003 he was thinking about lines. He drew a line on a map that ran through Nottingham, England, and Belfast, Ireland. Anyone who lived on that line, he announced, could write to him and request he come visit and make a pot of soup. The requests started coming, and he started visiting. During one particularly busy patch he made 11 soups in 7 days.

Drummond was bitten by the soup bug at a Belfast arts festival in 1998. He'd been asked to contribute to the event, but rather than produce something generally recognized as art, he decided to cook soup for 30-odd artists. He documented the whole thing in a story called "Making Soup" (published in a collection called *45*).

When you're making soup, he writes in "Making Soup," you can lose yourself. "The imagination can start to spiral into uncharted regions, reality can become bearable, even enjoyable."

The Soup Line is driven by the idea that a line—typically a device used by mapmakers and governments to divide people, segregating them into counties or states or nations—can be turned into a means of fostering community by bringing people together around a pot of soup. To further that end, he provides a poetical set of instructions on creating a Soup Line at penkilnburn.com/soup.

The soup is basically done. You can let it ride as is, or you can throw a couple of pounds of mussels in and let them cook in the soup. Microplane a lemon or two in there, it's brilliant. Before you serve it, toss in a bunch of basil, stir through, and that's it. Ladle it out, Parm it up, drape it with lardo, slivered cerignola olives, whatever. It's good.

Gabe McMackin has been cooking for a long time. He's worked in lots of restaurants with lots of great people. He lives in Brooklyn.

# PIZZA SOUP
*from*
## LACEY SWAIN AND DEREK ERDMAN

The secret of pizza soup, says Lacey, is that there is no secret—and no actual recipe: "Make it how you like. Fly by the seat of your pants. It's pizza. It's soup. It's Pizza Soup, and it has endless variations, but this is mostly how I made it." She and her housemate Derek Erdman contributed it to Soup & Bread in Seattle, to resounding applause. It was, said a fellow cook, "An idea whose time has come."

## INGREDIENTS                    SERVES 16

- **2** large onions
- **1½** pounds white mushrooms
- **2** heads of garlic
  basil, oregano, and Italian parsley to taste
- **2** pounds Italian sausage, crumbled into bits
- **2-3** 15½-ounce cans tomato sauce
- **2-3** 15½-ounce cans diced tomatoes
  medium to large wedge of Parmesan
- **2** cups shredded mozzarella

## PREPARATION

Sauté the onions, mushrooms, spices, and garlic in a big pot until the onions look good to you and your house smells awesome. Next, add the sausage and brown it up a little. Dump in all the cans of tomato stuff.

Be careful that the consistency of what you've got going on stays thinner than, say, spaghetti sauce, because that's basically what you're making. You want to be able to say with a straight face, "Have this bowl of pizza soup!" rather than, "Here is a weird bowl of something that should have noodles under it!" Chances are you might need to throw some water in there to make it soupier.

After you've let this simmer for an hour or so go ahead and grate that entire wedge of Parmesan straight into the pot. Ladle the soup over a slice of crusty bread placed in the bottom of your bowl, and top with mozzarella and red pepper flakes. Ta-da!

Lacey Swain is an anagram for "always nice." She was born and raised in Texas and eventually moved to Seattle, where she lives with her husband Ruben, two cats named Larry and Frampton, and a dog named Chuy Pancakes. Lacey has been described as a "social building block" and is really good at cooking without guidance.

Derek Erdman is (his words) a chubby only child who acts like an only child and runs a free psychic hotline.

# CIABATTA
*from*
## LA FARINE BAKERY

One of my favorite parts of Soup & Bread is stopping by La Farine Bakery, in Chicago's West Town neighborhood, to pick up the day's haul of bread. Rida Shahin and his staff have been stalwart supporters, donating bags of rolls, baguettes, and this award-winning ciabatta every week. If you live in Chicago and don't feel like trying your hand at this yourself, get on over to Chicago Avenue and grab a loaf. It is amazing.

This recipe requires a dough mixer such as a KitchenAid 5-quart, a 3-gallon plastic bin, a clean spray bottle, and a cooling rack.

**INGREDIENTS**                      MAKES 3 LOAVES

SPONGE STARTER
- ¼ teaspoon dry yeast
- 3 cups water

CIABATTA
- sponge starter
- 5 cups Gold Medal all-purpose flour
- 1½ cups water
- 1¼ teaspoons active dry yeast
- 3 teaspoons salt
- olive oil
- sea salt

**PREPARATION**

SPONGE: Mix ¼ teaspoon yeast in 1 cup warm water and stir until dissolved. Take ¼ cup of the mixture and dissolve into 2 cups of water. Let ferment at room temperature for 4 hours, then put in fridge overnight.

CIABATTA: The next day, combine sponge, yeast, flour, and 1 cup of water (reserve the other ½ cup for later) in mixer. Mix for 5 minutes on speed setting 2 (slow). Let dough rest for 20 minutes. Add salt. Mix for 4 minutes on speed setting 4 (faster). Slowly add ½ cup of remaining water until mixture absorbs water, mixing on speed setting 2.

After all the water is absorbed, mix dough at speed setting 4 for 1 minute. Mixture will be very sticky. Let ferment for 1 hour in a plastic container 3 times larger than the amount of dough. Expect dough to grow 3 times its size as the day progresses.

After 1 hour dust a clean kitchen counter with flour. Pour dough mixture onto counter and fold in the top of dough into the center, fold in the bottom of dough onto center, fold in the right side of dough into center, and fold in the left side of dough into the center. Return to plastic container. Let rest for 1 hour.

Dust countertop with flour again, and punch and fold several times. Return dough to plastic container. Let rest for 1 hour.

Dust counter top with flour again, and again punch and fold a few times. Return dough to plastic container. Let rest for 8 hours or overnight.

Preheat oven to 450°F for 1 hour.

Cut dough into 3 equal-size pieces and shape into oblong loaves. Place on baking stone. Spoon olive oil across top, making sure to cover it thoroughly. Sprinkle each loaf evenly with sea salt. Bake 35 minutes or until golden brown.

During baking use a spray bottle to squirt water onto the baking stone to make steam. Do this every 10 minutes or so, and close oven door immediately after to contain steam in oven. This gives the ciabatta a nice, crispy crust.

Let stand 20 minutes after baking on a cooling rack. Enjoy!

La Farine Bakery, located in Chicago's West Town neighborhood, was voted "Best Bread" in the city by *Chicago Magazine* in 2010. La Farine bread is available for purchase at the retail location and for wholesale accounts; see lafarinechicago.com

# OLIVE CIABATTA
*from*
## LUKE JOYNER

Feeling creative? Try this variation. Luke brought some of these loaves fresh out of the oven to Soup & Bread. He used the basic ciabatta recipe in Rose Levy Beranbaum's *Bread Bible*, but it works with the La Farine recipe here as well.

## INGREDIENTS

MAKES 1 LOAF

ciabatta dough
¼–⅓ pound pitted kalamata olives

## PREPARATION

Follow directions for ciabatta (page 109). When dough has risen three times, turn it out onto a slightly oiled counter, divide into thirds, and shape one hunk (handling as little as possible) into a long rectangle.

Place half the olives on one third of the rectangle, and push them into the dough slightly. Fold that third over onto the middle third of the rectangle. Place the remaining half of the olives atop the now double-height middle portion. Fold the final third of the dough over this, so that you have a dough/olive/dough/olive/dough sandwich. Poke the top of the dough down with your fingers. Push in the sides of the dough slightly. Repeat this poke/push maneuver a couple times.

Flip the dough over onto a sheet tray lined with parchment paper. Cover with oiled plastic wrap, and let rise again, about 1 hour in a slightly warm place.

Preheat your oven to 475°F. If you have multiple sheet trays, put one in the oven as you preheat. Put a pan that can withstand high heat on the floor of the oven.

When ready to bake, remove the plastic wrap, brush the surface of the bread with olive oil, and sprinkle a little salt on it. Put the bread into the oven, nesting its tray in the sheet tray that's already in there. Throw two handfuls of ice cubes into the pan on the floor of the oven, and quickly close the door.

After 5 minutes, reduce heat to 450°F. Continue baking for 20 minutes. Turn the oven off, and open the door halfway for 5 minutes before removing the bread.

Transfer bread to a wire rack to cool. Eat and enjoy!

Luke Joyner is a graduate student in architecture at the University of Michigan, with special interests in the intersection of architectural design and urban social issues—but before moving to Michigan, he lived in Chicago, where he ran marathons and programs for high school students and worked as a cook and freelance graphic designer.

# CHAPTER SIX

# Soup for Spreading the Word

While Upton Sinclair was researching *The Jungle*, the muckraking 1906 novel that exposed the grisly dangers of the Chicago stockyards, he often stopped for dinner in the Residents' Dining Hall at Hull-House, the pioneering settlement house on Chicago's near west side. Gertrude Stein dined there as well, as did W.E.B. DuBois and Ida B. Wells—and hundreds of impoverished recent arrivals from Italy, Greece, Poland, Lithuania, and beyond.

Driven to improve immigrants' chances at a creating a better life in Chicago, Hull-House founder Jane Addams and fellow crusaders for social justice agitated against child labor and for safe housing and sanitary working conditions, and their settlement house provided a social outlet for all comers. Hull-House volunteers offered classes in literature and art, presented lectures and plays, served dinner and staged dances. And when they realized industrial workers nearby had nowhere to get a hot, healthy lunch, they brought the food to the factories—trucking over vats of soup from the Hull-House kitchen and offering a bowl, plus a piece of bread and a cup of coffee, for just five cents.

They could have just started a soup kitchen, but Hull-House was never a charity, explains Lisa Lee—the executive director of what's now the Jane Addams Hull-House Museum on the campus of the University of Illinois at Chicago. "They expected people to donate something in return, whether it was their cultural capital, their social capital, or just the five cents. It was not a place where they were giving handouts.

"That's where we came up with the name 'Re-Thinking Soup,'" she adds. "Because it was about rethinking what it means to serve soup for free in world where people say there is no free lunch."

Inspired in equal parts by Hull-House's legacy of outreach and by the dictum of Slow Food guru Carlo Petrini that says engaged citizens should be "co-producers" of the food they eat, the museum's Re-Thinking Soup program offers a free lunch of soup served every Tuesday in the museum's Arts-and-Crafts-style dining room. But there's more on the menu than split pea.

Each week the museum offers programming designed to spark conversations about food, sustainability, nutrition, politics, and community. Speakers have included farmers and foodies, academics and activists. One week there might be a film on water preservation, another a beekeeper speaking on colony collapse disorder. Artist Sarah Kavage spoke in 2010 about her project tracing the role of the commodity wheat market in the global food system. At her Hull-House talk she gave away five-pound bags of flour and urged recipients to cook with it, share the food with others, and then get back to her with news of what had become of it. (You can find Sarah's recipe for veggie chili on page 90.)

Another Tuesday had standing-room only for a presentation on food deserts—neighborhoods whose primary food sources tend toward convenience stores and fast food outlets. The dining room's long refectory tables were covered with brown butcher paper and set with pertinent reading matter, such as Joan Dye Gussow's *This Organic Life* and Marion Nestle's *What to Eat*. Some lunchers, opting to take their carrot-ginger soup sans PowerPoint, carried their bowls outside and dined al fresco.

Carrot-ginger soup had been on the menu for the very first Re-Thinking Soup as well. The carrots came from far away—Mexico maybe, or Chile—and were a strategic choice made to help facilitate discussion of the difference between local and organic foods, help diners understand the concept of food miles and, in the words of Hull-House food preservationist Tara Lane, "show how the carrot relates to us all."

Lee and Lane came up with Re-Thinking Soup with another pro, Sam Kass, who bowed out in 2009 when he moved to Washington, D.C., to continue serving as the Obama family's personal chef and to take a new position as the administration's senior policy adviser for healthy food initiatives. He's famous now, the face of Michelle Obama's White House vegetable garden and her campaign for healthy food for kids, but in the early 2000s Kass and Lane worked together at Blackbird, a Michelin-starred restaurant that's not so far from Hull-House as the crow flies but culturally miles away. (See page 166 for a recipe from Blackbird owner Paul Kahan.)

Kass was a line cook and Lane was the executive pastry chef, but both were interested in the bigger food picture, looking for ways to develop as activists and educators. "I wanted to stay in the conversation about food," says Lane, "but I wanted to shift my focus to what was happening around food justice issues and farming and the distribution of local food. I was tired of spending endless hours just cooking."

Lane, Kass, and Lee dug into the history of the settlement house and specifically its dining room, looking for ways to link food to Hull-House's mission. What they came up with was soup.

A museum is so much more than a repository of artifacts, says Lee. "As cultural institutions we should be sites that foster radical democracy, that encourage dissent and conversations."

*In this chapter you'll find 12 recipes for soups showcasing the pure flavors of seasonal vegetables, as well as a recipe for a nutty harvest wheat boule. All the soup recipes can be turned vegetarian—just swap out the chicken stock or dashi for vegetable stock—and many can be tweaked to be vegan as well: just substitute olive oil where it calls for butter.*

Lee felt that standard models of museum programming—lectures, gallery talks—had become a bore. "We were sick of doing, like, 'here's the microphone'-type events," she says. The historic dining room, built in 1903, had been off-limits to the public, but Lee got it opened up. "It's a dining hall, we have a kitchen, maybe we should actually be eating in it, you know?"

"When we first started it we just said, 'Lets just make a pot of soup and see what happens,'" says Lane. "We knew what we wanted to do, but we didn't know how it would translate. I mean, we didn't even know if people would show up!"

They showed up: UIC students and staff, curious members of the food community, and others on the hunt for a hot lunch. A guy who works on the university's facilities staff told me he tries to come every week, "for the camaraderie, and because you learn about good foods and gardening—because they're right, the food we eat sucks."

Nowadays Lane is in charge of programming. Her sister Jessica, the Hull-House chef, handles the weekly soup, whose ingredients are often dictated by the harvest at the Hull-House farm a block away. The farm grows garlic, kale, tomatoes, cauliflower, and more, primarily as an educational enterprise.

"We use it as a teaching tool for telling the story of Jane Addams," says Lane, citing a well-known bit of Addams lore, in which an Italian neighbor introduced the reformer to a novel bulb called garlic, which she used to season a strange gravy of meat, cheese, and tomatoes over noodles.

Back then, the Hull-House Diet Kitch-en (as it was known) was offering cooking demonstrations and lessons on how to make hearty New England fare such as gruel, mutton broth, and flax seed tea.

That bowl of garlicky pasta Bolognese helped Addams realize that food was critical to understanding the immigrant experience. "It helped her come to grips with cultural difference," says Lee, "and with the potential for bridging that difference—she realized that it was one potential avenue for social transformation."

Lane and Lee took Re-Thinking Soup to San Francisco in 2008 for Slow Food Nation's celebration of American food, and to a museum conference in England in 2010, where they made 50 gallons of soup in one of Jamie Oliver's kitchens and

# Community Soup Night

Chicago's famously a "city of neighborhoods," and in 2010 Logan Square may have been the fastest changing 'hood in town. Its limestone three-flats and modest single-family houses were gentrifying, and the long-established Latino community was grappling with an influx of young professionals drawn by the neighborhood's affordable real estate and amenities like a farmers' market and sustainably focused restaurants.

When Noah Stein, a community gardener and urban farming activist, saw the changes in the neighborhood where he was raised, he decided to bring people together to talk about ways to cultivate a "responsible and responsive" food system. The means? Soup, of course.

Noah joined forces with Megan Larmer, who's part of a group lobbying to plant a community orchard on an empty neighborhood lot. They held their first Community Soup Night in February 2011 at Logan Square Kitchen, a shared-use commercial kitchen just up the street from a bustling new brewpub and down from the site of the proposed orchard. Soup ingredients were donated by the local Dill Pickle Co-op grocery.

"Join other gardeners, entrepreneurs and good food advocates in a healthy bowl of vegan minestrone and conversation about resource sharing, gardening and increasing community land for growing food in Logan Square," said the invitation. "Soup Night is meant to be a space for folks to network and build relationships, as well as foster hearty dialog about food, health and community space."

That first night around 40 diners shed their shyness and sat down to talk about ways to keep Logan Square friendly to urban agriculture and indie food enterprises. The second gathering, a month later, was so mobbed the soup ran out after 20 minutes. Stein was thrilled. "The pace of the city is driven, literally, at high speeds and causes us to be disconnected in unhealthy ways," he says. "Soup night's a way of slowing people down in much the same way as the work to build community gardens."

Want to brainstorm an issue at your own community soup night? Talk to a local restaurant about using their space on an off-night. See if you can get ingredients donated by a friendly grocer. And then spread the word.

trucked it to the Victoria and Albert Museum as part of a talk about how museums can foster social change.

"We don't want to treat the visitors here as just consumers of information," says Lee. "Our value as human beings has been reduced to our value as consumers, and for us it's like, well, how do you really value people as sentient human beings—as feeling, thinking, tasting, desiring human beings?"

# INSPIRATION KITCHENS' SWEET POTATO SOUP

*from*

## DAVID ROSENTHALL

This rich sweet-potato puree is the house soup at Inspiration Kitchens-Garfield Park, a café and job-training program that's the latest addition to Chicago-based Inspiration Corporation's network of initiatives addressing homelessness and poverty. On its own the soup is clean and simple; dress it up with the crema and pepitas if you're feeling fancy.

**INGREDIENTS**                    SERVES 12

### SOUP

- **2** pounds sweet potatoes, peeled and cut into 1/2-inch pieces
- **4** tablespoons butter
- **1/2** tablespoon light brown sugar
- **1/2** tablespoon fresh grated ginger
- **1** leek (white and pale green parts), thinly sliced
- **2** ribs celery, chopped into 1/2-inch pieces
- **6** cups vegetable stock
- **3/4** cup orange juice
- **1** cup heavy cream
- **1** tablespoon salt
- **1/2** teaspoon white pepper

### CUMIN CREMA

- **1** cup sour cream
- **2** tablespoons cream cheese
- **1** teaspoon ground cumin
- **1** tablespoon lime juice
- **1** tablespoon cilantro (chopped)
- **1/2** teaspoon salt
- **1/4** teaspoon white pepper

### TOASTED PEPITAS

- **1** cup raw pepitas (pumpkin seeds)
- **1** teaspoon salt
- **1/2** teaspoon pepper
- **1/4** teaspoon ancho chili powder
- **1** tablespoon olive oil

**PREPARATION**

SOUP: Melt butter in large pot over medium heat then add sweet potatoes and sugar and toss to coat. Add leeks, celery, salt, and pepper and sauté for 15–20 minutes. Add stock, juice, and cream and bring mixture to boil. Reduce heat and simmer until ingredients are very tender, 30–45 minutes.

Puree soup and, if necessary, return soup to pot. Thin with more broth, if desired. Season with salt and pepper.

Serve garnished with cumin crema and toasted pepitas.

CUMIN CREMA: Combine all ingredients in food processor and pulse until thoroughly incorporated.

TOASTED PEPITAS: Combine ingredients in bowl and toss to coat. Spread seeds out on a parchment-lined sheet tray and toast in 350°F oven, turning occasionally, until lightly browned, approximately 15–20 minutes.

David Rosenthall is executive chef at Inspiration Kitchens-Garfield Park, a food-service training program that helps Chicagoans affected by homelessness or poverty to learn culinary skills and pursue a career in the hospitality industry. Learn more at inspirationkitchens.org.

# ROASTED BEET SOUP

*from*

## CLEETUS FRIEDMAN

Cleetus brought this stunning soup in 2011 — a beet soup with the magical power to send a seven-year-old boy back for thirds. "I grew up, like most kids, disliking beets," he says. "But when I started committing to cooking seasonally, I ran into the dreaded beet season. This made me start working with them and having more fun with them. These days, beet soup is not only one of my favorites, but something that will convert those like me into beet lovers, too."

### INGREDIENTS                      SERVES 8

- ¼ pound red beets (about 3 medium)
- ¼ pound golden beets (about 3 medium)
- 1½ teaspoons butter
- 1½ teaspoons olive oil
- 1 leek, chopped
- 1 small onion, thinly sliced
- 1 celery stalk, chopped
- ⅛ teaspoon ground ginger
- ⅛ teaspoon ground allspice
- ⅛ teaspoon ground white pepper
- 2 cups water
- 1 small bay leaf
- 1 fresh thyme sprig
- 1 fresh parsley sprig
- ¼ cup whipping cream
- 2 tablespoons sour cream
- 1 small smoked trout

**PREPARATION**

Preheat oven to 350°F. Wrap beets in foil and roast until tender when pierced with fork, about 1 hour. Cool.

Peel beets. Cut ¼ of 1 beet into ¼-inch cubes; reserve for garnish. Cut remaining beets into ½-inch pieces.

Melt butter with oil in heavy medium saucepan over medium-high heat. Add leek, onion, and celery and cook until beginning to brown, stirring frequently, about 13 minutes. Stir in ginger, allspice, white pepper, and ½-inch beet pieces. Cook until vegetables begin to stick to bottom of pot, stirring frequently, about 7 minutes.

Add 2 cups water, bay leaf, thyme sprig, and parsley sprig. Bring to boil. Reduce heat to low, cover, and simmer until vegetables are very tender, about 25 minutes. Strain soup through a chinois, then cool slightly. Puree soup with cream and season to taste with salt and pepper.

Garnish with sour cream and shredded smoked trout, if you like.

Cleetus Friedman is the owner of City Provisions, a catering and events company and delicatessen showcasing local, sustainable food and drink.

# YELLOW WINTER VEGETABLE SOUP
*from*
## MELISSA YEN

Melissa coaxed stunning amounts of rich, full flavor out of this deceptively simple pot of carrots, sweet potatoes, and rutabagas. It was very satisfying, and the sunny color is enough to perk you up on the gloomiest of winter days.

## INGREDIENTS                    SERVES 8–10

- **3** carrots, coarsely chopped
- **2** sweet potatoes, peeled and coarsely chopped
- **1** rutabaga, peeled and coarsely chopped
- **2** Granny Smith apples, peeled, cored, and coarsely chopped
- **10** cups chicken or vegetable stock
- **1** teaspoon salt
- **½** teaspoon black pepper
- **1** stick of butter, softened
- **¼** teaspoon freshly grated nutmeg
- **1** tablespoon chopped fresh rosemary
- **6** green onions, sliced
- **1** teaspoon paprika

## PREPARATION

Place the carrots, sweet potatoes, rutabaga, and apples in a big pot and cover with chicken stock. Stir in the salt and pepper. Place over medium-high heat and bring to a boil.

Cook until vegetables are very tender, about 25 minutes. Drain and reserve stock. Return cooked vegetables to the pot.

Add butter, nutmeg, and rosemary. Roughly mash veggies with a potato masher until chunky. Return the stock to the pot and bring to a low simmer. Season with additional salt and pepper to taste.

Ladle into bowls and garnish with green onions and paprika.

Melissa Yen is the owner of Jo Snow Syrups, a Chicago company making small-batch artisanal syrups for coffee, snow cones, Italian sodas, and cocktails.

# SUNCHOKE SOUP
*from*
## SOHUI KIM AND BEN SCHNEIDER

Sohui and Ben were among the first New Yorkers to sign on when we made a road trip to hold a Soup & Bread at the Brooklyn club the Bell House in 2010. That event was a blast—with 9 cooks and more than 200 attendees we raised $900 for the New York City Coalition Against Hunger—but the raucous dinner we had the following night at their restaurant, the Good Fork, was just as memorable. This soup showcases the sweet, nutty flavor of sunchokes—tubers more commonly, and confusingly, known as Jerusalem artichokes. It's refined, but still earthy—and while Sohui and Ben served it with just chopped chives, Sohui suggests garnishing it with anything deep fried: oysters, shrimp, shaved and fried sunchokes, or potato chips. You get the idea.

## INGREDIENTS
SERVES 8

- **12** cups water
- **1** lemon
- **2½** pounds sunchokes
- **2-3** tablespoons butter
- **1** large onion, medium dice (1½ cups)
- **4** cloves garlic, roughly chopped
- **1** large leek, white part only, medium diced (1-1½ cups)
- **2** large Yukon gold potatoes, large dice (2 cups)
- **12** cups vegetable broth or dashi
- salt and pepper
- **½** cup heavy cream (optional)

## PREPARATION

Peel sunchokes and cut into 1-inch slices. Place in a pot and cover with water and lemon juice to keep them from oxidizing while you're cooking the rest of the soup.

In a large stockpot, sauté onion, garlic, and leeks in butter until soft and translucent, then add potatoes and drained sunchokes. Cook a few minutes more, then add broth or dashi. Puree, then add cream and salt and pepper to taste.

Ben Schneider is a longtime theater actor/carpenter turned restaurateur who joined forces with his chef wife, Sohui Kim, to create the Good Fork in 2006. They live in Red Hook, Brooklyn, a block away from their restaurant, with their two children Jasper and Oliver.

# 40-WATT GARLIC SOUP
*from*
## ROBIN LINN

When this soup turned up at Soup & Bread, frankly, we were wary. But after giving it a try we were struck by how much potent garlic flavor this soup delivered without being the least bit bitter. Robin warned that garlic overload might hit later in the evening, but I at least suffered no ill effects. In fact, I credit this soup with staving off a nascent sore throat. We present it h5ere in honor of Jane Addams and her garlic epiphany.

**INGREDIENTS**                    SERVES 8

- **40** garlic cloves, 1 reserved and thinly sliced
- **2** tablespoons olive oil
- **2** tablespoons butter
- **2¼** cups roughly chopped onions
- **1½** teaspoons chopped fresh thyme
- **1** sage leaf
  dash of cayenne
- **¼** cup dry sherry
- **3½** cups chicken or vegetable stock
- **½** cup heavy cream or milk
- **1** cup finely grated Parmesan cheese (half for serving)
- **½** loaf French-style bread, ripped up, crusts removed
  lemon juice to taste
  salt and pepper

## PREPARATION

Preheat oven to 350°F. Place all but one garlic clove in glass baking dish. Add olive oil and sprinkle with salt and pepper; toss to coat. Cover baking dish tightly with foil and bake until garlic is golden brown and tender, about 45 minutes. Cool. Squeeze garlic between fingertips to release cloves from husks. Set aside.

Melt butter in large, heavy saucepan over medium-high heat. Add onions and cook until translucent, about 5 minutes. Add thyme, sage, garlic slices, cayenne, and a dash of salt. Cook until onions begin to brown. Add sherry, scraping up any brown bits. Add roasted garlic and stock. Cover and simmer about 20 minutes.

Add half the bread and cook for a couple of minutes. Turn heat off, and puree soup until smooth. Add remaining bread as needed to thicken. Return to heat, add cream or milk, and bring to a simmer. Season with salt and pepper and add half the Parmesan.

Before serving add lemon juice to taste and any desired extras, such as chopped spinach or escarole, croutons, garlic chips, cooked pasta, or minced chives.

Serve topped with remaining Parmesan. Enjoy!

Robin Linn produces Chicago Public Radio's music talk show, *Sound Opinions*. She often brings huge containers of soup with her to work, and if you're nice, she'll share.

# LEEK SOUP
*from*
## KRISTIN BASTA AND GUY MASSEY

Vegetarian Kristin and meat-eating Guy collaborated on this silky soup—adapted from an *Epicurious* recipe. Kristin says they were going for something really simple to balance out some of the more showy soups that were turning up at Soup & Bread, but they also liked that they could customize it to many tastes by adding a little hot harissa, a North African chile paste, or a bit of crème fraiche, or even, yes, some bacon. "Pick yer poison," she says. Sound advice.

**INGREDIENTS**                          SERVES 6

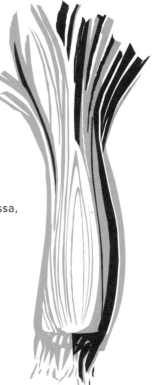

- **8** medium leeks or so (about 3 pounds), white and pale green parts, chopped
- **1** medium onion, chopped
- **1–2** carrots, chopped
- **2–3** celery ribs, chopped
- salt and black pepper
- **1** stick unsalted butter
- **2** small thin-skinned potatoes
- **½** cup dry white wine
- **3** cups roasted vegetable stock (they used Chuck's, found on page 190)
- **3** cups water
- **1** bay leaf
- **1½** cups fresh flat-leaf parsley leaves, chopped
- **¼** cup all-purpose flour
- crème fraiche or chilled heavy cream, hot harissa, or bacon (cooked and chopped) on the side

## PREPARATION

Wash sliced leeks in a large bowl of cold water, agitating them, then lift out and drain well in a colander.

Cook leeks, onion, carrot, celery, salt, and pepper in 4 tablespoons butter in a large, heavy pot over moderate heat, stirring occasionally, until softened, about 8 minutes. Peel potato, if you feel like it, and cut into ½-inch cubes, then add to onion mixture along with wine, stock, water, and bay leaf. Bring to a boil, then reduce heat and simmer, partially covered, until vegetables are quite tender, about 15 minutes.

Stir in parsley and simmer uncovered another 5 minutes. Discard bay leaf and keep soup at a low simmer.

Melt remaining 4 tablespoons butter in a heavy 1-quart saucepan over moderate heat, then add flour and cook roux, whisking, until golden, about 3 minutes. Remove from heat and add 2 cups simmering stock (from soup), whisking vigorously (mixture will be thick), then stir or whisk mixture into remaining soup and return to a simmer, stirring well.

Puree soup until smooth, about 1 minute per batch, transferring to a 4-quart saucepan. Reheat if necessary, then season with salt and pepper.

Serve soup as is, or topped with whipped cream—if you'd like a dollop, beat heavy cream in a chilled bowl with an electric mixer at medium speed until it almost forms soft peaks—or creme fraiche, or whatever strikes your fancy. Kristin thinks it's tasty with a couple of dashes of harissa; Guy likes his with bacon.

Guy Massey acts and Kristin Basta takes pictures; both are members of Chicago's Theater Oobleck.

# ROASTED ONION SOUP
*from*
## SARAH STEEDMAN

I first encountered this simple soup when Sarah brought it to Bonnie's soup swap (see page 28). She reprised it several weeks later, in early March, for Soup & Bread. She'd wanted to make something seasonal, she said at the time, but just about the only thing in season at the end of a Chicago winter are the onions and potatoes left lurking in the root cellar. Note: the Gruyère croutons lend this soup (which Sarah adapted from a *Bon Appétit* recipe) a passing resemblance to the French standard, but the roasted onions give it a deeper, sweeter flavor.

## INGREDIENTS                    SERVES 8
- **8** tablespoons butter, divided
- **24** cups thinly sliced onions (about 5¾ pounds)
- **8** cups (or more) low-salt chicken or vegetable broth
- **1½** cups multigrain bread, cut into ½-inch cubes
- **¾** cups coarsely grated Gruyère
- **3** tablespoons fresh thyme leaves, divided
- **1½** tablespoons (or more) white wine vinegar

## PREPARATION

Melt six tablespoons butter in an extra-large heavy pot over medium-high heat. Add onions, sprinkle with salt and pepper and sauté until onions begin to soften, 15 to 18 minutes. Reduce heat to medium and sauté until onions are very tender, stirring often and adjusting heat as needed, one hour longer.

Preheat oven to 375°F. Toss bread cubes with cheese, one tablespoon thyme and two tablespoons melted butter, season with salt and pepper and spread on a rimmed baking sheet. Bake until cheese has melted and bread is lightly crisp, about 10 minutes. Let cool.

Add eight cups broth to onions in pot and bring to boil. Add two tablespoons thyme. Reduce heat and simmer 25 minutes to blend flavors. Cool slightly. Puree soup until smooth. Return to pot and add more broth by ¼ cupfuls to thin soup to desired consistency. Season to taste with vinegar, salt, and pepper.

Sprinkle with croutons to serve.

Sarah Steedman lives in the West Walker neighborhood of Chicago with her husband, Chris, two energetic young girls, Sophia and Charlotte, and little whip of a dog, Gretl. She's an urban organic gardener, an aficionado of Mexican and Japanese food, and a maker of stuffed animals from scraps of fabric.

# MEXICAN CORN SOUP

*from*

## MARK AND HEATHER FERGUSON

This soup balances the sweet crunch of corn (frozen is fine but fresh is amazing) with the smoky heat of roasted poblanos, bringing them into harmony in a nice, big pot of milk. And while all those garnishes do entail some extra work, the added value they bring to the bowl is worth the effort. Isn't everything better with avocado and cheese?

### INGREDIENTS

SERVES 8

- 2½ cups frozen or fresh corn
- 4½ cups milk
- 1 medium onion, small dice
- ¼ cup butter
- salt and pepper to taste
- 2 cups vegetable stock (more or less as needed)
- 2-3 roasted poblano peppers
- fried corn tortilla strips or chips
- Monterey jack, pepper jack, or queso fresco
- cilantro
- avocado

### PREPARATION

Thaw corn and dice onion. Using tongs, roast poblano peppers on stove top (for gas burners) or in broiler until black on the outside, then place on a plate under a bowl (to cool (this steams the skin, making it easier to remove).

Melt butter in stockpot and sauté onion until translucent; sprinkle with a little salt to sweat onion. Add corn, milk, and vegetable stock to stockpot, then blend until smooth. Bring to a boil and reduce to a simmer for about 15 minutes. If you don't have an immersion blender, take the corn, 1 cup of milk, veggie stock (as needed), and onions and blend in blender until smooth. Pour corn mixture back into stockpot and add the rest of the milk and bring to a boil, then simmer for 15 minutes.

Take peppers and gently remove skin, seeds, and stems. Slice into thin strips or small dice, shred cheese, and dice avocado.

Place peppers in soup bowl and pour soup over peppers. Garnish with tortilla strips, avocado, cheese, and cilantro.

Mark and Heather Ferguson own Hard Boiled Records in Chicago's Roscoe Village neighborhood.

# THE COLOR OF MONEY PEA SOUP
*from*
## SUSANNAH KITE STRANG

This quick-and-easy pea soup requires less than half an hour of prep time—unless you go the distance and shell two pounds of fresh peas, in which case, says Susannah, "I would just sauté them in butter, sprinkle them with chopped mint, and forget the soup!" Fresh or frozen, this soup delivers a straight shot of vibrant spring-pea flavor. And the color is gorgeous: serve in pretty cups with a jaunty drizzle of crème fraiche and a dot of Sriracha to impress your friends.

**INGREDIENTS**                    SERVES 6–8

- **3** tablespoons butter or olive oil
- **2–3** shallots, chopped
- **1** large or 2 small leeks, cleaned and sliced
- **2** pounds shelled fresh or frozen peas
- **1** teaspoon salt
- **1** teaspoon sugar
- **8** cups water
- **1** large handful flat leaf parsley
- **1** small handful fresh mint
  additional salt, white pepper, sugar, to taste
  lemon, crème fraiche, and/or Sriracha as desired

**PREPARATION**

Heat the butter in a soup pot until foaming, then sauté the shallots and leeks until soft. Pour in the peas, and cover to thaw (skip this step if using fresh peas). Once thawed, remove the lid and sauté for 5 minutes, until the peas are plump and thoroughly hot. Add the teaspoon each of salt and sugar as the peas are cooking.

Pour in the liquid, bring to a boil. Reduce heat, tear up the parsley and mint and toss in. Simmer all together for 5 minutes or so.

Use a food mill or blender to puree the soup in batches. Alternatively, finely chop shallots, leeks, and herbs prior to adding, and use a potato masher to create a more textured soup. Return the blended soup to the pot, and reheat to just below a simmer. Add additional seasonings to taste.

Serve plain, with lemon, or topped with crème fraiche and/or Sriracha as desired.

Susannah Kite Strang is an artist and high school teacher whose allergies include penicillin, gin, and Mr. Bubble.

# CAULIFLOWER AND WATERCRESS SOUP
*from*
## MAGGIE KAST

Maggie describes this soup as "a compromise between the classical French *Potage de la Fontaine Dureau* transmitted by Julia Child and the vegetable puree soups developed by *Cook's Illustrated*. For a large quantity, or if you must hold off on serving, puree the watercress separately with a cup of cold soup and add to the hot at the last minute, to preserve the color."

### INGREDIENTS SERVES 6-8

- **1** head cauliflower, 1½–2 pounds
- **1** cup chopped onion, leek, or a combination thereof
- **2** tablespoons butter
- **2** tablespoons flour
- **½** teaspoon ground coriander (optional)
- **1** cup or more whole milk
- **¼** cup heavy cream
- **1** bunch watercress, washed, stems discarded, roughly chopped
  salt and pepper to taste

### PREPARATION

Break cauliflower into florets and peel central stem, keeping any tender leaves. Melt butter and sweat onion over low flame until soft. Add flour and stir a few minutes until it starts to stick. Add 2 cups water and cook, stirring until it thickens and comes to a boil. Simmer a few minutes. Add cauliflower (not leaves), optional coriander, 1 teaspoon salt, and 2 more cups water, and cook 20–25 minutes, until cauliflower is easily pierced with a fork. Add leaves and watercress and cook just until greens turn bright. Puree and add milk, using more if needed to obtain desired consistency. Season to taste with salt and pepper. Add cream and serve.

Maggie Kast is the author of *The Crack Between the Worlds: A Dancer's Memoir of Loss, Faith, and Family.*

# FENNEL SOUP WITH A SWIRL
*from*
## BONNIE TAWSE

Up until she was 30 or so, Bonnie hated fennel because it smelled like black licorice, which she loathes. But one summer afternoon, her brother-in-law made her a mess of sliced fennel that he caramelized and then sprinkled with shaved Parmesan. "I took a bite just to be a nice person," she says, "and then had one of those transformative food moments. I said, 'Wait, this is fennel? This is amazing.' And since that afternoon I've been happy to try fennel in all sorts of preparations. I have a lot of lost time to make up." She got this recipe from a friend of a friend who heard about her soup swap (page 28) and hit her up at the gym to talk soup; it's adapted from *Heart of the Artichoke*, the cookbook by Chez Panisse chef David Tanis.

## INGREDIENTS                    SERVES 6

### SOUP
¼ cup olive oil

3 medium fennel bulbs, trimmed (reserving fronds), cored and cut into very thin slices

half of a large white onion, thinly sliced

2 shallots, thinly sliced

4 medium cloves garlic, coarsely chopped

salt and freshly ground black pepper

¼ cup (raw) long-grain white rice

6 cups chicken or vegetable broth

### SWIRL
1 cup coarsely chopped fennel fronds (from the fennel bulbs)

leaves from 4 to 6 stems flat-leaf parsley, chopped (½ cup)

1 teaspoon capers, drained

½ cup packed basil leaves

¼ cup chopped scallions, white and pale green parts

½ cup olive oil

salt and freshly ground black pepper

## PREPARATION

Heat the oil in a large heavy-bottomed pot over medium heat. Add sliced fennel, on-ion, shallots, and garlic. Season generously with salt and pepper. Cook for about 15 minutes, stirring often, until mixture has softened and picked up a little color. Add the rice and the 6 cups of broth. Increase the heat to medium-high. Bring to a boil, then reduce the heat to medium-low. Taste and adjust seasoning as needed. Cook for 20 minutes.

Puree soup and then strain through a fine-mesh strainer into the pot that was used to cook the soup; discard any fibrous solids. Set pot over medium-low heat. If the consistency of the soup is too thick, add broth as needed.

While the soup is warming, make the green swirl: Rinse and dry your blender, then add the fennel fronds, parsley, capers, basil, scallions, oil, and salt and pepper to taste. Puree on high speed until smooth, then transfer to a small bowl. Ladle equal portions of soup into individual bowls. Swirl a tablespoon of the green puree into each bowl.

Bonnie Tawse is a wife, mama, ethnic food freak, and urban nature explorer.

# SPRINGTIME SIMPLE SORREL SOUP
*from*
## TERRA BROCKMAN

Terra Brockman cut the sorrel for her tangy spring soup, adapted from Patricia Wells's *Bistro Cooking*, straight from the soil at her brother Henry's organic vegetable farm. She's intimately familiar with that soil, and in 2009 turned her observations of its rich history and potential into a memoir, *The Seasons on Henry's Farm*. It's a great book—thanks both to Terra's lyrical writing and the mass of useful information on cooking and farming she packs into her graceful prose.

### INGREDIENTS                    SERVES 4-6

- **8** ounces fresh spring sorrel
  salt and freshly ground black pepper
- **6** cups water
- **1** pound potatoes, peeled and cubed
- **2** eggs
- **¾** cup heavy cream or crème fraiche

### PREPARATION

Unless the sorrel is very young, remove the stems and central ribs. Combine the sorrel and a few teaspoons of water in a large saucepan over low heat. Stir from time to time as the sorrel wilts down to an olive-green puree. Add 6 cups of water and salt and pepper to taste. Bring to a boil. Add the potatoes and cook over low heat until potatoes are soft, 15–20 minutes. You can leave the potatoes as chunks, or blend it if you want a smooth soup.

Combine the eggs and cream or crème fraiche in a warmed soup tureen or serving bowl. Mix until well blended. Add a ladle of the potato-sorrel mixture and blend well to gently warm the egg/cream mixture. Pour in the remaining potato-sorrel mixture. Stir and serve immediately, topped with more crème fraiche.

Terra Brockman is the fourth of five generations of a central Illinois farm family. She is a speaker and author, and the founder of the Land Connection, an educational nonprofit working to ensure that more Illinois farmland will grow local foods for our tables; for more see terrabrockman.com.

# HARVEST WHEAT BOULE
*from*
## ANNE KOSTROSKI

Anne's known on the Chicago bread scene for her open-minded approach to baking, incorporating everything from apples and walnuts to hot dogs and celery salt into her artisanal loaves. She sells at Chicago farmers' markets and a few select retail outlets under the moniker Crumb Chicago—and she's brought the extras by the Hideout on a few happy Wednesdays. Use this simple no-knead bread as the foundation for your own creative experiments.

## INGREDIENTS
MAKES 1 BOULE

- 1⅝ cups lukewarm water
- ⅛ teaspoon yeast
- 2⅝ cups organic unbleached bread flour
- 1 cup organic whole wheat flour
- ⅓ cup organic oat flour
- ¼ cup organic cracked wheat
- 1 teaspoon and a pinch kosher salt

## PREPARATION

Combine water and yeast to dissolve yeast. Add remaining ingredients. Mix ingredients until thoroughly combined. If dough appears dry, begin to add water in small increments until dough resembles a very thick batter.

Allow dough to rest for 12 hours in a warm environment (preferably close to 70°F). You will see bubbles on top of dough after 12 hours, which signal the dough is ready. Turn out dough onto counter and begin kneading until a round boule develops. Place dough onto a floured towel and then cover. Allow dough to rise again for 2 hours.

To see if dough is ready to bake, gently press your finger into the side of boule. If it bounces back quickly give the dough another 15–20 minutes. If it bounces bake slowly then you are ready to bake.

Half an hour before baking turn oven on to 400°F. Place your Dutch oven into oven to begin heating up. Place boule into cooking vessel and cover. Bake for 20 minutes and check to see if top is brown. If so, remove lid and continue baking until boule is golden brown.

After working around the country in restaurants and bakeries, Anne Kostroski returned to the Midwest and to her true passion—baking bread.

# CHAPTER SEVEN

# Soup for Peace

"The first time we got artichokes," said Jenny Abrahamian, "we got a huge box, and they just sat there—because nobody knew what they were, or how to cook them!"

That problem, at least, had been solved when Jenny and I, along with a half dozen other women, made our way through a large box of the confounding thistles, in the kitchen of a community arts center in Chicago's Humboldt Park neighborhood. Outer leaves and stems were discarded; the tender innards were roughly diced and tossed into a colander to be turned into artichoke soup.

"*Mira, mira,*" said one of the cooks, as the others gabbed away in Spanish, "*No es bueno, si?*" She pointed to an artichoke heart still coated with a hairy "beard," indicating that it still needed to be cleaned.

"*Si,*" I agreed. "That's no good."

The chokes, a bit past their prime, had been donated by Whole Foods to the Humboldt Park chapter of Food Not Bombs, which meets every Saturday in the Rumble Arts Center's ramshackle kitchen to prepare and serve a free meal.

On the floor were more boxes, of potatoes and pears and bananas, and some markedly bruised eggplant. In addition to the soup, the day's menu included fruit salad, brown bread, and roasted root vegetables. All of it vegan, and—with the exception of a few spices and oils—all of it made from donated or "rescued" food.

Aside from the church, Food Not Bombs may be one of the longest running sources of free soup in the world. The first Food Not Bombs action took place in Boston in 1981, when a group of antinuclear activists dressed as Depression-era hobos gave away soup made from discarded produce to protest the business interests behind a nuclear power plant. According to *Food Not Bombs: How to Feed the Hungry and Build Community*, a history of the movement, more than 100 people showed up that day.

The Boston group's actions, which continued through the 80s, combined street theater and antiwar politics with free meals to convey their message that food is a human right. As the decade rolled on, the idea spread to other cities—notably San Francisco, where in 1988 volunteers were repeatedly arrested for serving food to the homeless in Golden Gate Park. The arrests gave the movement a national profile and over the next 20 years an estimated 1,000 Food Not Bombs chapters have popped up around the world.

People come to the group from different backgrounds and with different agendas: Some might be antiwar activists, others are motivated by food politics, or animal rights, or hunger and homelessness. Membership is open to all, but every collective operates according to some basic principles: rescue and redistribute vegetarian food that would otherwise go to waste (in actions called "serves"), promote solidarity with other social justice causes, and get out in public and make a spectacle of yourself.

That last requirement has made Food Not Bombs a reliable presence at antiwar marches and rallies. Robert Clack, a community organizer and antiglobalization activist, first encountered the group at the 2002 World Economic Forum in New York City and was impressed to see it a year later in Chicago during the march against the invasion of Iraq that shut down Lake Shore Drive. "I really appreciated the solidarity of having someone be there with free food and this message of peace," he says.

Robert and a handful of others founded the Humboldt Park chapter in 2006; their first serve was at a rally commemorating the 2003 protests. They started dishing up soup and salads from a picnic table in the park that gives the neighborhood its name a month later, cooking at a nearby church whose outreach focused on the rights of immigrant day laborers.

A serve isn't quite the same as the work of a traditional soup kitchen. "We are political—what we do every week is a protest against the misappropriation of resources in our society," says Robert.

Another founding member, Brad, says, "We try to make the politics evident but not mandatory—not like a soup kitchen where you might have to say a prayer before you eat."

Neither Robert nor Brad is actively involved with the chapter anymore—as they both pointed out, the logistics of democratic consensus building can be exhausting. At the Rumble Arts Center, a long-haired man named Mark offered this take: "We're not trying to be a charity, we're doing justice," he said, citing San Francisco's legendary Diggers. The food is free, said Mark, because it belongs to no one and everyone. "It's free because it's yours." (For more on the Diggers see page 151.)

Jenny, a 30-year-old chemist with a day job in a research lab, had been volunteering with the chapter since shortly after it started up. In college, she said, she "was involved in every activist group around, but then I graduated and sort of settled into this adult life of going to work every day, and I got very detached. I felt really removed from other kinds of activism and wanted to find something that worked for me."

Jenny was the designated "bottom-liner" the day I was there—the Food-Not-Bomber charged with making sure everything got done. As we cooked, more people showed up with donations from the local food co-op. In addition to the cooked food, the chapter also gives away groceries each week, and soon boxes of produce and bags of day-old bread and pastries lined the floor.

This particular chapter used to be "more a bunch of punk kids," Jenny said. Nowadays, it's more diverse and community-based, and "closer to the ideal." Of the group gathered, more than half were Latino. Most of them had found out about the chapter through its weekly serves in the park and had started to come out to help cook when activity moved indoors for the winter. The rest were a mix of volunteers from a Christian group home, people from the arts center, and, sure enough, a crusty punk or two.

*You won't necessarily have to try hard to "make it work" with the 12 vegan soup recipes that follow. And if you want to go all the way, there's a recipe for some toothsome vegan bread as well.*

"This is going to be…interesting," said Jenny, poking a wooden spoon at a pan full of artichoke hearts sizzling along with some olive oil and onion on the stovetop.

There wasn't any vegetable stock in the kitchen, so while I wrestled the artichokes into a rickety blender, Jenny whipped up an impromptu bouillon by mixing Italian seasoning mix into a pot of simmering water. It was salty but serviceable, and after mixing in the artichoke puree we set the pot on a long table along with the fruit salad, bread, and potatoes. After people packed tote bags with the slightly worn groceries, they stopped for bowls of soup and plates of veggies before heading home with their haul.

Some Food Not Bombs chapters create elaborate menus, but Jenny, dipping into her bowl, said "We're sort of more *Iron Chef* about it. Like, here are your ingredients—just make it work."

# ROASTED ROOT VEGETABLE SOUP
*from*
## GRACE TRAN

When Grace said she was bringing a soup built on roasted root vegetables to Soup & Bread, I was expecting heavy-duty winter starches like sweet potatoes and turnips. Instead, this soup is full of light and sprightly parsnips and celery root, mixed with earthy nutmeg and the surprise of spinach. Roasting the roots first brings out the sugar and helps build fantastic flavor in the pot.

**INGREDIENTS**                    SERVES 12

- **2** tablespoons extra virgin olive oil
- **1** large onion, thinly sliced
- **2** leeks, white and pale green parts, thinly sliced
- **2** garlic cloves, minced
- **1** cup pearled barley
- **8** cups low-sodium vegetable broth
- **4** cups water
- **10** thyme sprigs
- **2** bay leaves
- **½** pound celery root, peeled and cut into ½-inch cubes
- **1** pound parsnips, peeled and cut into ½-inch pieces
  salt and freshly ground pepper
- **1** pound baby spinach
- **1** teaspoon freshly grated nutmeg

**PREPARATION**

Preheat oven to 400°F. Toss celery root and parsnips with olive oil. Roast for 35–45 minutes, until caramelized. Stir occasionally.

In a large pot, heat the oil. Add onion, leeks, and garlic and cook over moderate heat, stirring occasionally, until tender, about 5 minutes. Stir in barley. Add vegetable broth, water, thyme and bay leaves, and bring to a boil. Add celery root and parsnips and season with salt and pepper. Simmer over moderately low heat until barley and root vegetables are tender, about 40 minutes to an hour.

Stir in the spinach and nutmeg and simmer for 5–7 minutes. Season with salt and pepper and serve in deep bowls, along with hearty whole-grain bread.

Grace Tran works with a counseling program at the non-profit Alternative Schools Network and is an organizer of the Chicago Youth Community Film Festival for high school students. In her spare time, she watercolors, draws comics, and enjoys fine films.

# POTATO, BUTTERNUT SQUASH, AND LEEK SOUP

*from*

## KENT LAMBERT

Kent swiped the combo of roasted butternut squash and coriander that makes this soup so distinctive from a recipe in the *Veganomicon*—Isa Chandra Moskowitz and Terry Hope Romero's comprehensive guide to successful vegan cooking—but then he freestyled, using it as a rather racy component in an otherwise staid potato-leek soup.

**INGREDIENTS**                    SERVES 16

- **1** medium butternut squash, peeled, seeded, and chopped into ¾-inch pieces
  olive oil
- **1** tablespoon crushed coriander
- **½** teaspoon salt
- **6** pounds purple and Yukon gold potatoes, peeled, pared, and chopped into ½-inch pieces
- **4** leeks, finely chopped
- **1** tablespoon ground black pepper
- **1** teaspoon rosemary
- **1** teaspoon thyme
- **1** teaspoon rubbed sage
- **1** tablespoon salt
- **16** cups vegetable stock
  chopped parsley

## PREPARATION

Place the squash pieces in a roasting pan, drizzle a little olive oil over them, and toss them with the coriander and salt. Roast in a preheated 375°F oven for an hour or more, until soft and a little bit caramelized. Remove from the oven and set aside.

Heat a tablespoon of olive oil in a soup pot over medium heat. Add the leeks, potatoes, herbs, and salt and sauté, stirring frequently, until the leeks are translucent and the potatoes are starting to brown. Add the soup stock and bring to a boil. Simmer for 15 minutes or so, until the potatoes are starting to get soft. Add the roasted squash. (Note: if you happen to have squash puree on hand, e.g., leftover from Thanksgiving dinner, you could just add it with some crushed coriander a few minutes after this point.)

Continue to simmer for another few minutes or until the squash is totally soft. Puree the soup and return to pot, if necessary. (If you're using squash puree, add it after pureeing the potatoes and leeks and stir by hand until the orange streaks have vanished.) Add more salt, if needed.

Garnish each serving with chopped parsley. A touch of lemon zest or juice with each serving brightens the soup nicely, as well.

When not cooking, baking, videomaking, or doing other hibernatory activities, Kent Lambert croons and plays keytar with his band, Roommate.

# RED PEPPER SOUP
*from*
## SWIM CAFÉ

The folks at Swim—a sustainably minded café in Chicago—have been great friends of Soup & Bread from the beginning. They've supplied many soups to our crocks and staff members have pitched in to help me set up tables, slice bread, and just generally keep an eye on things. Choosing just one of their soups for this book was rough. But this one was so powerfully bright, it would have been criminal not to share it. The crisp flavors of red pepper and asparagus play cheekily off the sweet base of coconut milk—an underappreciated staple of vegan cooking, at least in my kitchen. After tasting this soup I vowed to forevermore give it the respect it deserves.

## INGREDIENTS

SERVES 8

olive oil
**2** tablespoons minced garlic
**3** red bell peppers
**1** celery stalk
**1** whole red onion
**2** cups vegetable broth
**3** 14-ounce cans coconut milk
juice of one lemon
**2** teaspoons coriander
**1** mint leaf, chopped fine
**7-8** basil leaves
**⅓** bunch asparagus
salt and pepper to taste

## PREPARATION

Heat olive oil until fragrant. Sauté garlic, 2 diced red peppers, celery, and onion in the oil, then add vegetable broth and blend until smooth. Add coconut milk, lemon juice, coriander, and herbs.

Roughly chop the remaining red pepper and, in a separate pan, sweat over low heat.

In a separate pot, blanch the asparagus, then shock the spears by immersing them in ice water to lock in the color. Chop into approximately 1-inch lengths.

Add the vegetables to the soup, season with salt and pepper to taste. Simmer 10 more minutes and serve.

Swim Café makes its soups from scratch every morning from fresh, seasonal ingredients and gets weekly inspiration from the Green City Market and the folks at Scotch Hill Farm.

# COCONUT-RED LENTIL SOUP
*from*
## SHARON BAUTISTA AND DIMITRA TASIOURAS

This deceptively simple lentil soup packs a complicated bunch of alluring flavors into each spoonful: nutty lentils, sweet raisins and coconut milk, peppery ginger, hot cayenne. Sharon and Dimitra adapted it from a recipe by whole-foods guru Heidi Swanson, author of *Super Natural Cooking* and proprietor of the website 101 Cookbooks.

### INGREDIENTS                    SERVES 8–10

- **1** cup yellow split peas
- **1** cup red split lentils (masoor dal)
- **7** cups water
- **1** medium carrot, cut into ½-inch dice
- **2** tablespoons fresh peeled and minced ginger
- **2** tablespoons curry powder
- **2** tablespoons coconut oil
- **8** green onions (scallions), thinly sliced
- **⅓** cup golden raisins
- **⅓** cup tomato paste
- **1** 14-ounce can coconut milk
- **2** teaspoons fine-grain sea salt
- **½** teaspoon (or more) cayenne pepper
  one small handful cilantro, chopped

### PREPARATION

Rinse split peas and lentils. Place in soup pot, cover with water, and bring to a boil. Reduce heat to a simmer and add the carrot and a half tablespoon of the ginger. Cover and simmer for about 30 minutes, or until the split peas are soft.

In the meantime, in a small, dry skillet or saucepan over low heat toast the curry powder until fragrant. Set aside. Place the coconut oil in a pan over medium heat, add half of the green onions, the remaining ginger, and the raisins. Sauté for two minutes stirring constantly, then add the tomato paste and sauté for another minute.

Add the toasted curry powder and cayenne to the tomato paste mixture, mix well, and then add this to the simmering soup along with the coconut milk and salt. Simmer, uncovered, for about 20 minutes.

Serve with cilantro and remaining green onions.

As Fork and the Road, Sharon Bautista and Dimitra Tasiouras lead off-the-beaten-path culinary bicycle tours around Chicago. There's more information at forkandtheroad.com.

# CURRIED SQUASH AND RED LENTIL SOUP

*from*

## WENDY DILLIARD AND MARIBETH HEERAN

A soup so nice, they made it twice! Wendy, a member of the culinary chat site LTH Forum, brought this squash-and-lentil concoction to Soup & Bread in 2010; Maribeth—another LTHer—whipped up her own rendition the following year. It's simple to make but tastes fancy and goes a long way toward rehabilitating the reputation of these at times maligned pulses.

### INGREDIENTS          SERVES 4–6

- **4** tablespoons vegetable oil
- **1½** pounds butternut squash, peeled, seeded and cut to a ½-inch dice
- **1** large onion, small dice
- **1** carrot, small dice
- **1** celery stalk, small dice
- **5** cloves garlic, minced
- **2–3** tablespoons ginger, minced
- **1** teaspoon salt
- **2** tablespoons curry powder
- **¼** teaspoon black pepper
- **1** cup red lentils, washed and picked over
- **4** cups vegetable stock
- **1** cup water
- **2** tablespoons lemon juice
- **½** cup vegetable oil
- **½** bunch cilantro, finely chopped

## PREPARATION

Heat oil over medium in a large Dutch oven. Add squash, onion, carrot, celery, garlic, ginger, and salt. Sauté until the vegetables soften and start to brown, 15–25 minutes. Add curry powder and pepper. Cook for 1–2 minutes.

Add lentils, vegetable stock, and water. Cover, reduce heat to simmer, and cook until lentils are done, or about 25–40 minutes. Add lemon juice.

Blend oil and cilantro. Garnish soup with cilantro oil.

Wendy Dilliard develops mobile products, applications, and solutions for business customers. Her German butcher grandfather would get a kick out of the fact that her first published recipe contains no meat.

Maribeth Heeran worked in restaurants for 15 years before working in commercial real estate. Concerned with both sustainability issues and supporting local food pantries, she's been writing on lthforum.com for a couple of years and has found it to be a wonderfully diverse community of people who are always available to help out when asked.

# CURRIED CARROT-GINGER SOUP
*from*
## SUZIE STRAIT

Suzie was the force behind Soup & Bread's 2011 foray to Seattle. She organized a soup extravaganza at the excellently divey Fun House, and lined up a bunch of bands to play afterward to boot. On top of all that, she had time to make this soup (adapted from a 2008 *Bon Appétit* recipe). Carrots and ginger are a classic combo, but the curry takes it to a new place altogether. Kind of like S&B and Seattle.

## INGREDIENTS                    SERVES 8

- **2** teaspoons coriander seeds
- **1** teaspoon yellow mustard seeds
- **3** tablespoons light sesame oil
- **1** teaspoon curry powder (preferably Madras)
- **2** tablespoon minced fresh ginger
- **2** cups chopped onions
- **1½** pounds carrots, thinly sliced into rounds (about 4 cups)
- **2** teaspoons finely grated lime zest
- **5** cups (or more) vegetable broth
- **1** 14-ounce can coconut milk
  fresh lime juice
  good extra virgin olive oil

## PREPARATION

Grind coriander and mustard seeds in spice mill to fine powder. Heat oil in a large, heavy pot over medium-high heat. Add ground seeds and curry powder; stir 1 minute. Add ginger; stir 1 minute. Add next 3 ingredients. Sprinkle with salt and pepper. Sauté until onions begin to soften, about 3 minutes.

Add broth and bring to boil, then reduce heat to medium-low and simmer uncovered until carrots are tender, about 30 minutes. Add coconut milk. Cool slightly. Puree until smooth and return to pot if necessary. Add more broth by the quarter cup if soup's too thick. Ladle into bowls and top with squeeze of lime and drizzle of good olive oil; season with salt and pepper.

Aspiring cookbook author Suzie Strait is a staunch believer in both soup and social justice.

# CHIPOTLE AND CUMIN BLACK BEAN SOUP

*from*

## GEMMA PETRIE

This hearty and flavorful soup pairs the rich kick of chipotles with tart lime juice and aromatic cumin—all of which play off the earthy, almost meaty flavor of plain old black beans. Tip: save the water that results from soaking your beans to make a batch of black bean broth, a restorative, antioxidant-rich drink said to be an excellent cure for gout.

### INGREDIENTS                    SERVES 10

- **16** ounces dried black beans, rinsed and picked over to remove any grit or stones
  water
- **1** tablespoon olive oil
- **2** red onions, chopped
- **1** red bell pepper, chopped
- **1** yellow bell pepper, chopped
- **1** green bell pepper, chopped
- **6** garlic cloves, minced
- **4** teaspoons ground cumin
- **2** canned chipotle chiles in adobo sauce, chopped (less for a milder soup)
  salt and black pepper
- **2** tablespoons fresh lime juice
  cilantro
- **½** cup sour cream (optional)

### PREPARATION

In a large pot, bring the dried beans and 7 cups of water to a boil. Reduce heat and simmer for 2–2½ hours, adding more water if necessary. Cook until the beans are tender. Salt to taste (salting earlier will cause the skins to toughen). Note: The beans can be prepared a day or two ahead. Allow to cool at room temperature and store in an airtight container in the refrigerator. If you prefer to use canned beans, substitute 7–8 cups—and do not drain.

In a second large pot, heat the oil over medium-high heat and add the onion and bell peppers. Cook until tender and beginning to brown, about 8 minutes. Add the garlic, cumin, and chiles and cook for 1 minute. Add the prepared beans. Cover and simmer for about 20 minutes. Season to taste with salt and freshly ground black pepper. Stir in the lime juice. Serve garnished with cilantro and, if you like, sour cream (though that'll make the soup no longer vegan).

Gemma Petrie studies library and information science and writes about food for Pro Bono Baker (probonobaker.com) and Gapers Block (gapersblock.com).

# SPICY VEGAN TORTILLA SOUP
*from*
## MICHAEL SLABOCH

This light and piquant pot is just one of several versions of tortilla soup in Michael's repertoire. "It started out with shredded chicken, chicken stock instead of water, and topped with avocados and cheese," he says. "But since many of my friends were vegan or vegetarian it morphed into this vegan recipe." It's also, he warns, pretty spicy—feel free to adjust chiles and peppers to taste.

**INGREDIENTS**                    SERVES 6

- **2** tablespoons canola oil
- **1** red pepper, seeded and chopped
- **1** green pepper, seeded and chopped
- **1** red onion, finely diced
- **2** cloves garlic, minced
- **2** tablespoons fresh oregano (or 2 teaspoons dried)
- **1** tablespoon cumin
- **1** tablespoon chili powder
- **2** jalapeno peppers, seeded and chopped
- **3** fresh tomatoes or 1 cup diced canned tomatoes with juice
- **4** cups cold water
  - juice from 1 fresh squeezed lime
- **1** can black beans, drained and rinsed
- **2** cups fresh or frozen corn kernels
  - fresh cilantro, chopped
  - fresh tortilla chips, crushed
  - kosher salt

**PREPARATION**

Heat the canola oil in a saucepan over medium-high heat. Sauté the red and green peppers, onion, garlic, oregano, cumin, and chili powder for 3 minutes, until the onion is translucent, stirring often. Add the jalapeno and tomatoes; continue stirring for one minute. Add the fresh lime juice and cold water.

Bring the soup to a boil, then reduce the heat and simmer uncovered for 20 minutes. Add the black beans and corn and return the soup to a boil. Remove the soup from the heat, put crushed tortilla chips in the bottom of each bowl, stir in the cilantro and season with kosher salt.

Michael Slaboch is a multimedia artist living in Chicago whose post-production sound work has been heard on many albums as well as on NPR, Animal Planet, the Discovery Channel, and the History Channel, and in feature films. He is also a producer and audio/visual archivist for the reissue label the Numero Group (numerogroup.com) and the talent booker at the Hideout.

# Soup for the 60s

The Diggers, an ad hoc group of guerrilla street-theater freaks, were the spiritual forebears of Food Not Bombs. Icons of the counterculture that rolled out across the land from San Francisco in the late 1960s, they took their name from a 17th-century group of English utopian, communist farmers and were the messy masterminds responsible for various happenings, including the famed Death of Hippie parade. They declared money an unnecessary evil; in the Diggers' alternative economy, everything was free—clothing, medicine, art, love, and, natch, food. The Digger archives (online at diggers.org) sketch out the vision of a "Free City," exhorting fellow travelers to "hit every available source of free food…and fill up their trucks with the surplus by begging, borrowing, stealing, forming liaisons and communications with delivery drivers for the leftovers from their routes." Every day in Golden Gate Park the group distributed stew made from scavenged food, and free whole-wheat Digger Bread, baked in coffee cans at their Free Bakery, became famous across the city.

The scene persisted into the 1980s—among the Digger archives is an anonymous first-person account of one man's short-lived experiment in serving free soup to the hippies and burnouts of the park's Panhandle in 1983. "When comes the time to leave this world someday," it concludes, "what you get to keep is what you gave away."

# BLACK BEAN, HOMINY, AND SWEET POTATO SOUP

*from*

## CAROL WATSON

This soup is inspired by classic Mexican flavors—cumin, black beans, smoky chipotle chiles, and fresh cilantro—and features hominy, a form of corn fairly underutilized outside of the southern U.S and Mexico. Hominy is hulled corn that's been stripped of its bran and germ. It has the flavor of corn but also a unique taste thanks to the lye solution it's soaked in to remove the hulls, and a slight chewiness because the corn is first dried and then rehydrated. "I think of this soup as the perfect comfort food for a fall weekend," says Carol. "Make it once and simply reheat anytime you feel like another bowl. It's even better the next day, after the flavors have had time to intensify."

**INGREDIENTS**                    SERVES 8

- 2 tablespoons olive or vegetable oil
- 1 medium yellow onion, chopped
- 1 jalapeno pepper, seeded and chopped
- 4 garlic cloves, chopped
- 1 large carrot, peeled and chopped
- 1 stalk of celery, chopped
- 2 teaspoons ground cumin
- 8 cups vegetable stock
- 1 large sweet potato, peeled and chopped into ½-inch pieces
- 1 29-ounce can hominy, drained and rinsed
- 1 14-ounce can diced tomato, drained
- 2 15-ounce cans black beans, drained and rinsed
- 3 canned chipotle peppers in adobo sauce, finely chopped
- 1 bunch of cilantro, roughly chopped
- 1½ teaspoons salt, or to taste
- ⅛ teaspoon pepper
- 1 avocado, peeled and thinly sliced
- 1 lime, halved, for garnish
- 2 cups tortilla chip strips, for garnish

## PREPARATION

Heat the oil in the bottom of a 6-quart stockpot or Dutch oven on medium heat. Add the onions and sauté until soft and translucent, about 4 minutes. Add the jalapeno and the garlic and cook on low until soft, another 2 minutes. Add the carrot and celery and cook until just soft, then stir in the cumin and cook a bit longer, until fragrant.

Add the vegetable stock. Bring to a boil, then reduce heat and add the sweet potato, hominy, tomatoes, and black beans. Simmer at low heat 40 minutes to an hour, or until the potatoes are soft.

Add the chipotles and cilantro. Season with salt and pepper.

Divide among bowls and garnish each with a slice of avocado, a squeeze of lime, and about a quarter cup of tortilla chip strips just before serving.

Carol Watson had been a managing partner at Chicago's Mia Francesca restaurants for 7 years when she decided to expand her culinary knowledge. She attended culinary school in San Francisco, then returned to Chicago and opened Milk and Honey Café.

# VEGAN POZOLE
*from*
## CYNDI FECHER

Vegan pozole? This was a first—and a tasty surprise. Who knew you could make posole without pork? "It isn't any less hearty as a result," says Cyndi, and, in fact, though she toyed with adding tofu or some other veggie protein, she ultimately abstained. "It seemed a little criminal," she said. "It really doesn't need it."

**INGREDIENTS**                    SERVES 8

- **25** tomatillos
- **1** white onion
- **3** medium tomatoes
- **2** jalapenos (add more for more heat)
- **1** tablespoon epazote (or use Mexican oregano if you can't find it)
- **1½** teaspoons cumin
- **8** cups hominy
- **1** small head garlic (more or less for taste)
  vegetable bouillon and water, or your favorite broth
  olive oil
  cilantro

## PREPARATION

This stew happens in a few steps—roasting, sautéing, pureeing, and then finally cooking it all together.

First, peel and halve the tomatillos and place them cut-side down in a roasting pan that has a little oil in the bottom. Wash and halve the tomatoes and peel and roughly chop the onions as well. Roast in a 375°F oven, covered, for about 40 minutes to an hour, or until they collapse.

Meanwhile, drain and rinse the hominy. Finely chop the garlic and jalapenos. Remove the seeds and ribs from the jalapenos if you want less heat in the soup, or omit them entirely. In olive oil, sauté the peppers and garlic until soft, around five minutes.

Add in the hominy, and a little more oil as needed. On top of the hominy, add in the dried epazote. Stir in the cumin and salt and pepper to taste. Go a little easy on the salt, as you'll be adding quite a bit of broth.

Check the veggies in the oven. If they've collapsed and are soft to the touch, they're ready. Take this opportunity to pull the skins off the tomatoes—no need to do it earlier. Then puree the tomatillos, onions, and tomatoes, and any liquid produced during roasting. Add roughly half a bouillon cube to each roasting pan of vegetables. Keep the veggie puree on low heat as the hominy continues to sauté with the spices.

After 10 minutes, add the vegetable puree to the hominy and spice mixture and simmer for about 10–20 more minutes. Thin out the soup with water or broth to your liking, adding more seasoning as necessary.

Serve immediately, topped with chopped cilantro. You can also garnish with thinly sliced radishes, a few cooked black beans, or some slivers of avocado.

Cyndi Fecher edits children's curricula by day and moonlights as a food blogger. You can find her at kitschandkin.tumblr.com.

# WEST AFRICAN SWEET POTATO, AND PEANUT SOUP

*from*

## SHARON BAUTISTA, CINNAMON COOPER, CLIFF ETTERS, ANDREW HUFF, ROBYN NISI, AND SHANNA QUINN

These folks are the brains behind the food-and-drink section of Gapers Block, a Chicago-based website focused on local news and events. The name comes from the traffic bottleneck caused by drivers rubbernecking at an accident, but it's meant as a reminder to slow down and appreciate the city. And that's a directive that applies just as well to soup. This soup has a hearty peanut flavor and a crazy, fluffy texture—almost like pumpkin pie filling, if it were made from sweet potatoes and peanuts.

## INGREDIENTS
SERVES 6–8

- **1** tablespoon olive oil
- **1** large white onion, chopped
- **6** cloves garlic, minced
- **3** carrots, chopped
- **2** large sweet potatoes, peeled and cubed
- **1** teaspoon salt
- **1** teaspoon cumin
- **1** teaspoon thyme
- **1** teaspoon smoked paprika
- **½** teaspoon turmeric
- **¼** teaspoon cinnamon
- **½–1** teaspoon hot sauce
- ground black pepper to taste
- **1** 15-ounce can diced tomatoes
- **6** cups vegetable broth
- **½** cup peanut butter
- **1** diced scallion

## PREPARATION

Place a large pot over medium heat. Once it's warmed, add the oil and the onions. Cook for 5–7 minutes. Add the garlic and cook for 1 minute. Add the carrots, sweet potatoes, and spices and stir thoroughly. Cook for 5 minutes and add a little broth if necessary to keep the vegetables from sticking.

Increase the heat to medium-high and add the can of tomatoes and the broth. Stir, including the bottom of the pan. Bring to a boil. Reduce the heat to low and let the vegetables simmer for 25–30 minutes. Use an immersion blender or potato masher to break up the potato chunks and make smooth.

Increase the heat to medium and stir in the peanut butter. Cook for 5 minutes until the peanut butter is thoroughly combined and warmed. Serve over rice with a sprinkle of scallion for garnish.

Drive-Thru (gapersblock.com/drivethru) is the food and drink section of Gapers Block, covering the city's vibrant dining, drinking, and cooking scene.

# PEANUTS O'TOOLE

*from*

## JEANINE O'TOOLE

Jeanine came up with this version of a classic African peanut soup after trying a couple of different recipes floating around out there. It's peanutty but nicely skirts the danger of tasting like...well...warm peanut butter. Add more red pepper if you like it extra spicy.

**INGREDIENTS**                         SERVES 10

- **2** tablespoons peanut oil
- **1** medium-large yellow onion, finely diced
- **3-4** large garlic cloves, minced
- **1** chili pepper, finely diced, with seeds, or 1 teaspoon red pepper flakes
- **3** celery stalks, diced
- **2** carrots, diced
- **1** red bell pepper, diced
- **1** 28-ounce can diced tomatoes with juice
- **8** cups mild vegetable broth (not too salty)
- **½** cup uncooked white rice
- **9** ounces creamy peanut butter (add more to make a rich stew)
  chopped roasted peanuts and/or chopped cilantro for garnish

**PREPARATION**

Heat oil in a large stockpot over medium-high heat. Cook onion, garlic, and chili pepper about 5 minutes. Add celery, carrots, and bell peppers. Stir in tomatoes with their juice, vegetable broth, and pepper. Simmer uncovered, for 10 minutes.

Add rice to soup and stir. Reduce heat, cover, and simmer until rice is tender, or about 20 minutes. Stir in peanut butter and return to a simmer until it blends in.

Serve garnished with chopped peanuts and/or cilantro.

Jeanine O'Toole is a musician from Chicago who enjoys reading cookbooks and writing vegan baking recipes.

# YEAST-FREE VEGAN BREAD
*from*
## RAE HILL

I confess, when I hear the words "vegan baking" I don't have high hopes. No butter to make the bread moist? No eggs to bind ingredients together? No honey to add a little something sweet? Yikes—and now you want to take the yeast out as well? Yet against all odds, this loaf is light and toothsome. The almond milk smooths out the rough edges, turning flour, salt, and oil into something genuinely delicious.

## INGREDIENTS

MAKES 1 ROUND LOAF

- **2** cups bread flour
- **1** cup whole wheat flour
- **4** teaspoons baking powder
- **1** teaspoon salt
- **½** cup almond milk or water (works with any liquid)
- **¼** cup olive oil (you can substitute melted milk-free margarine, vegetable oil, or any other liquid fat)

## PREPARATION

Preheat oven to 400°F.

Mix all dry ingredients together and set aside; in a separate bowl, combine almond milk or water and the oil. Pour liquids into the dry mixture, then stir just until the flour is incorporated and you can no longer see dry granules. Depending on the humidity of the air where you live you may need a little bit more or less liquid. The dough should be moist but not sticky.

Let the dough sit for 3 or 4 minutes to allow the flour to fully absorb the liquid—do not rush to add more liquid or flour, and make sure not to overstir the dough or your bread will be tough.

Dust a baking sheet with flour, then oil your hands; this will keep the dough from sticking to them. Shape the dough into a ball and place on baking sheet. Score the surface in a diamond or X shape to prevent splitting of the crust.

Bake for 40 minutes; let cool and serve.

Rae Hill resides in Chicago, where she's living the dream with her husband Todd and working as a pastry chef.

# CHAPTER EIGHT

# Soup that Shines

As demonstrated throughout this book, soup is a frugal way to feed a crowd. It's peasant food. It's home cooking. It's fuel for starving artists. What it's not, plainly, is fancy. I mean, c'mon, who goes to a four-star restaurant panting for *soup?*

Well, Andrew Zimmern, for one. In 2010 the host of Travel Channel's *Weird Food* series pegged an "explosively vegetal" beaker of freeze-dried, deconstructed pea soup at Chicago's avant-garde Alinea as the best thing he'd eaten anywhere in the city. An elaborate construction of pale-green powder set off by gelled pearls of honeydew, olive oil, and burrata, it was, he said, "just for flavor alone...like diving into a pea pod."

Of course, not every professional chef is busily alchemizing honeydew nectar into pellets as garnish for his freeze-dried soup. It takes a battalion of sous chefs and a closet full of high-tech gadgetry to produce such cutting-edge results. But the pros who have participated in Soup & Bread have plenty of tricks up their sleeves.

Paul Kahan, chef and owner of a quartet of acclaimed Chicago restaurants, emulsifies egg yolk with a hot caramel sauce as a topping for a garbanzo bean soup he serves—with pickled Asian pears—at Blackbird, the fanciest of the four. There's no special technology required but, he allows, "it's not really something you would do at home."

Something you could do at home, though, is add truffles to your split-pea soup, as Kahan did for a pot he brought to Soup & Bread. "It's a very easy tweak," he says. "It's one of the simplest, most frugal soups out there, just strained to a fine texture and fancied up in presentation." (See page 166 for the recipe.)

Luxury ingredients like truffles have long shown up in soup, from the country club standard of lobster bisque to the ethically compromised Chinese delicacies of shark-fin and bird's nest soups. Even jewels have found their way into the pot: one 15th-century French recipe for medicinal broth calls for the steeping of a cloth pouch containing gems such as rubies, emeralds, and pearls.

But of course, rubies—and truffles—can cost. Luckily, in soup, a little can go a long way. In fact, says Susan Goss, chef and co-owner of Chicago's West Town Tavern, soup is the restaurateur's "secret weapon." For soup a chef can use bits and pieces of whatever's lying around the kitchen, then incorporate a pinch of something pricey to take that soup from humble to haute. Take the extra step of passing a puree through a strainer a couple of times and you'll be rewarded with a velvety texture lush enough to satisfy the most exacting diner—all you need is the luxury of time. Susan's recipe for wild mushroom soup with decadent blue cheese croutons is on page 36.

Time is also the secret ingredient in Rob Levitt's preposterously potent lamb stock, the base for his simple but flavorful Scotch Broth. Levitt, proprietor of The Butcher and Larder, a sustainable butcher shop in Chicago, simmered the odd bits and bones of many lambs over many weeks, reducing the stock over and over again to build a concentrated base that, when he was done, he said, "was like caramel when you heated it up." This technique isn't for everyone—the recipe on page 176 is adapted for home cooks—but it produced a truly remarkable depth of flavor. "The idea is to take these 'food of the masses' concepts," he says, "and then apply the principles of fine cooking."

Stephanie Izard, winner of *Top Chef*'s fourth season and owner of Chicago's Girl and the Goat, is on board with this approach as well.

"There's nothing fancy about any of the ingredients we use," she says. "But when you put them together you can get an amazing bunch of flavors in one bite. You don't need to use expensive stuff as long as you prepare it well and put it together in a fun way and pay attention to contrast."

For Soup & Bread Izard concocted a pear, parsnip, and pistachio soup that was at once sweet, savory, nutty, and surprisingly hot, thanks to a dash of Thai chilies. With a puree like this as a base, you can then let your creativity run wild. "Garnishes are what make a soup stunning and give it layers of texture and flavor and can surprise people," she says. "It's so important to make your whole mouth happy." The recipe for this alliterative wonder, along with directions on preparing its garnishes of romesco sauce, preserved lemons, and garlicky crunch, starts on page 170.

But wait, you may well be asking. What does all this restaurant cooking have to do with building community? For explanation I'll turn to Hugh Amano, a professional cook who lost his job a few years back and launched a blog called Food on the Dole, dedicated to teaching himself, and others, how to eat like a king on a commoner's budget.

The recipe for his Pork Dumpling Gang soup (page 180) gives Stephanie Izard's soup a run for the prize for most elaborate in this book, with a perhaps overwhelming number of pieces and parts to assemble, including cured pork belly, pickled mushrooms, tortellini, and broth. But though the preparation may look daunting, it's quite simple once you break it down.

Cooking is the great equalizer, where history and tradition share the stage with creativity. And where working stiffs and fancy-pants gourmands can get their hands dirty using the same tools and techniques and produce similar results, all in service of the common goal of nourishing families and friends. "Everyone's got to eat," says Hugh. "If we can nudge the satisfaction of this need back in the direction of eating, sharing, and enjoying food together, and away from the 'food is a nuisance—give me a meal replacement bar' direction, I think that's a good thing."

"It makes people feel good to eat soup," says Susan Goss. "So if they're eating soup that's luxurious, whether that's achieved through texture or ingredients, it makes them feel twice as good."

In the 1987 film *Babette's Feast*, a penniless Frenchwoman living in exile wins the lottery, and blows her windfall on a preposterously lavish meal for the aged and pious townsfolk of her grim Danish village. She prepares turtle soup and quail in puff pastry and gets the teetotaling guests tipsy on the finest Burgundy. Under the meal's spell, old grudges are aired and forgotten, long-lost loves are forgiven their sins. And everyone totters back to their huts softened up by an indelible shared memory.

Babette, it's revealed, was once a celebrated Parisian chef (and a revolutionary who fled France with the fall of the Paris Commune). But her hospitality, like that proffered by great home cooks around the world, is born of love and generosity. Regardless of their circumstances expert cooks, professional and amateur, craft shared moments that can foster feelings of warmth and well-being. In their hands, whether you're sitting down with strangers at a friend's house or snagging a seat at an exclusive hot spot, you'll feel, for that meal, like part of the community.

*Following are recipes for nine soups that go the extra mile, whether through the use of (mildly) extravagant ingredients or the application of (somewhat) more advanced culinary techniques. Whip these out when you really want to make someone smile—and serve with some airy Parmesan-cheddar gougères or an elegant boule laced with onion jam.*

# CHEVRE BISQUE
*from*
## TAMIZ HAIDERALI

With its rich red hue and robust flavor, this soup was a staple on the Valentine's Day menu at Tamiz's cozy restaurant, Treat, which closed in 2011. Top it with crab meat or lobster and you've got something truly seductive.

## INGREDIENTS

SERVES 6

- **12** ripe Roma tomatoes, diced
- **2** tablespoons canola oil
- **½** cup chopped Spanish onion
- **¼** cup basil
- **3** tablespoons minced garlic
- **¼** teaspoon cayenne
- **6** cups water
- **½** cup goat cheese
  salt and pepper to taste
  basil chiffonade
  crab meat, lobster, and/or chives (optional)

## PREPARATION

Heat oil in a thick bottomed pan and sweat onions. When onions are translucent, add garlic and sauté until garlic takes on a golden color. For a robust garlic flavor, cook the garlic longer (recommended).

Toss in ½ of the basil and cayenne and stir for 30 seconds. Add the tomatoes and water and bring to a boil. Turn down heat and let simmer for 20 minutes. When tomatoes are fully cooked, add goat cheese and stir until fully integrated.

Remove from heat, add remaining basil, and puree.

Serve warm with garlic toast points and a chiffonade of basil, or top with warm crab meat, lobster, and/or chives as desired.

Tamiz Haiderali, a veteran of the Chicago restaurant scene, is the former chef/ owner of Treat Restaurant.

# BLACKBIRD'S YELLOW SPLIT PEA SOUP

*from*

## PAUL KAHAN

Chicago's multitasking star chef (at this writing he's got four restaurants and is plotting to open a butcher shop) took possibly the humblest of poor-man's soups, turned it into something utterly luxurious, and gamely dished it up for us at Soup & Bread surrounded by jazz musicians and other cooks of dubious repute. He said later that Soup & Bread was the most fun event he'd done all year.

**INGREDIENTS**                      SERVES 6–8

- ½ pound yellow split peas
- 4 tablespoons unsalted butter
- 2 ounces smoked bacon, diced
- 1 smoked ham hock
- 1 medium white onion, peeled and sliced
- 1 leek (white part only), washed, cut into ¼-inch slices
- 1 carrot, trimmed, peeled, washed and cut into ¼-inch pieces
- 1 garlic clove, peeled and crushed
- 3 cups light chicken stock
- 3 cups water
- 1 bouquet garni (1 bay leaf, 3 sprigs thyme, 4 large sprigs parsley, tied together with string or wrapped in a little piece of cheesecloth) salt and fresh ground pepper
- 3 slices white bread or brioche, crusts removed, cut into ½-inch cubes
- ½ cup heavy cream
- ½ tablespoon chervil leaves truffles (optional)

## PREPARATION

Wash the split peas in several changes of cold water then soak them in cold water for 2 hours. Drain and set aside.

In a large saucepan, melt 2 tablespoons of butter. Add the bacon and ham hock and sauté over medium heat for 4 minutes. Add the onion, leek, carrot, and garlic and sauté over low heat for 3 more minutes. Add the split peas, the stock and water, bouquet garni, salt and pepper to taste. Bring to a boil and simmer over low heat, covered for 1½ hours.

While the soup is simmering, melt the remaining 2 tablespoons of butter in a skillet and add the diced bread; sauté until golden brown. Drain the resulting croutons on a paper towel and set aside.

When the soup has cooked, remove the bouquet garni and ham hock; puree the soup for about 2 minutes or until smooth. Return soup to pot (if necessary) and bring to a simmer, then stir in the cream. Taste and adjust salt and pepper if necessary. Sprinkle with the chervil and serve hot with the croutons.

Note: Ham hock can be shredded or chopped and added to finished soup if desired.

Soup can be garnished with fresh or preserved truffles, thinly sliced, over the top.

Paul Kahan is a citizen, fisherman, gardener, and music lover, and executive chef of Chicago restaurants Blackbird, Avec, the Publican, and Big Star.

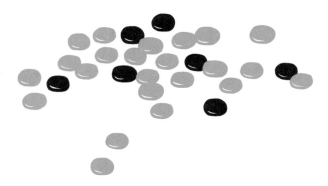

# CREAM OF ARTICHOKE SOUP

*from*

## RAE HILL

Rae came across this refined soup while perusing an old church recipe book passed down to her by her grandmother Margie. With their leafy armor and prickly core, artichokes are a challenge—and to the uninitiated the paltry yield of edible parts may not seem worth the fight to excavate them. But once you've tasted the tender, fleshy heart it's obvious why the funny-looking choke is a delicacy prized by cooks (and it's a potent source of antioxidants as well). The ingredients are fairly simple, but when this soup is strained to a lush, silken smoothness it's at home in the finest china.

**INGREDIENTS**          SERVES 8

- 5 large artichokes
- 7 tablespoons butter
- 1 medium leek, white and pale green parts, sliced and rinsed
- 6 garlic cloves, chopped
- 1/2 cup chopped shallots (or yellow onion)
- 8 ounces Yukon gold potatoes, peeled and diced
- 12 cups vegetable or chicken stock
- 1/2 bay leaf
- 2 sprigs thyme
- 4 sprigs of parsley
- 1/4 teaspoon cracked black peppercorns
- 1/2 cup cream
  salt to taste

## PREPARATION

Cut the artichokes lengthwise into quarters. With a small knife, remove the thistle choke part and discard. Cut away the leaves from the artichoke heart and reserve for steaming and eating later. Cut or peel away the tough outside skin of the stems and discard. Thinly slice the hearts or chop to a quarter-inch thickness.

In a large pot, melt half of the butter and cook the artichoke hearts, leek, garlic, and shallots on medium heat until tender but not brown. Add the potatoes and stock. Tie up the bay leaf, thyme, parsley, and peppercorns in cheesecloth and add to the pot. Increase heat to bring to a high simmer, then lower heat and continue to simmer uncovered for 1 hour.

Remove and discard the herbs. Puree the soup and pass it through a fine strainer—more than once, if desired. When ready to serve, heat the soup and whisk in the remaining butter and the cream. Season with salt and serve.

Rae Hill resides in Chicago, where she's living the dream with her husband Todd and working as a pastry chef.

# PEAR, PARSNIP, AND PISTACHIO SOUP
*from*
## STEPHANIE IZARD

This recipe from Stephanie Izard, Top Chef winner and chef-owner of the celebrated Chicago restaurant Girl & the Goat, may have been the most elaborate one ever served at Soup & Bread. Both Izard and Heather Shouse, her collaborator on *Girl in the Kitchen: How a Top Chef Cooks, Thinks, Shops, Eats, & Drinks*, showed up to do the honors. The sweetness and texture of the pears and parsnips work well together, the pistachios add a nice salty note, and the Thai chile offers a spicy contrast to the fruit. The servers even provided directions for whipping up the garnish of preserved lemons, romesco sauce, and crunchy garlic. Elaborate—and delicious.

**INGREDIENTS**            SERVES 4–6

SOUP

| | |
|---|---|
| **1** | tablespoon butter |
| **⅓** | cup diced yellow onion |
| **2** | garlic cloves, sliced |
| **½** | pound parsnips, peeled and sliced |
| **2** | Anjou pears, peeled, cored, and diced |
| **½** | cup white wine |
| **½** | cup roasted, salted pistachios, plus ¼ cup for garnish |
| **1** | dried Thai red chile |
| **3½** | cups chicken stock |
| **1** | cup milk |

PRESERVED LEMONS            ABOUT 1¼ CUPS

| | |
|---|---|
| **9** | lemons |
| **2¼** | cups coarse salt |
| **2** | cups sugar |
| **1½** | cups vodka |
| **1** | teaspoon fennel seeds |
| **1** | teaspoon whole black peppercorns |
| **1** | teaspoon red pepper flakes |
| **1** | teaspoon mustard seeds |

### ROMESCO SAUCE

- **1½** pounds Roma tomatoes, halved lengthwise, seeds removed
- **12** cloves garlic
- **¾** cup extra virgin olive oil, plus 2 tablespoons
- **2** ounces cubed ciabatta
- **2** ancho chiles, rehydrated in water, stems removed
- **⅓** cup almonds, toasted
- **⅓** cup hazelnuts, toasted
- **1** cup minced onion
- **½** cup white wine
- **¾** cup chopped parsley
- **1** teaspoon red pepper flakes
- **1** teaspoon paprika
- **2** cups chicken stock
- **1** ounce bittersweet chocolate
- **1** tablespoon brown sugar
- **1** teaspoon sherry vinegar
- **1** teaspoon soy sauce

### GARLICKY CRUNCH

MAKES 2 CUPS

- **2** cups fine bread crumbs
- garlic oil
- butter
- salt and pepper

### PREPARATION

SOUP: Melt butter over medium heat in a medium soup pot. Add onions and garlic and sweat until translucent.

Stir in pears, parsnips, and pistachios. Add white wine and reduce by ¾.

Add Thai chile, stock, and milk, bring to a boil; reduce heat and simmer for an hour.

Puree, then divide the soup among 4 or 6 bowls and garnish with pistachios, lemons, drizzle of romesco sauce, and a dusting of crunchy garlic.

PRESERVED LEMONS: Bring a large pot of water to a boil with ¼ cup of the salt. Boil half of the lemons for 5 minutes. Remove them with tongs and set aside to cool. Add the remaining lemons to the boiling water for 5 minutes, and then remove them and set them aside to cool with the others.

In a small pot, combine the remaining salt, the sugar, vodka, fennel seeds, peppercorns, red pepper flakes, and mustard seeds. Set over low heat and simmer for 15 minutes or until the sugar has dissolved.

Meanwhile, cut the cooled lemons, running your knife from just below the top of the lemon to just above the bottom, so as to cut into quarters without cutting all the way through the fruit. Stuff the lemons into a large glass jar with a lid (at least half-gallon-sized). Pour the salt liquid over the lemons, pushing the fruit down to make sure it's submerged. Let the liquid come to room temperature and then close the lid tightly. Let the lemons sit at room temperature for 2 weeks, then they are ready to use. (The preserved lemons can be refrigerated for up to 6 months. Use them anytime you need to add tartness to a dish, or wherever a recipe calls for lemon zest.)

ROMESCO SAUCE: Preheat the oven to 400°F. Line up the tomatoes, skin-side up, in an 8x8-inch baking dish. Tuck the garlic cloves in among the tomatoes, and drizzle with ¾ cup olive oil. Season with salt and pepper. Transfer the baking dish to the oven and roast until the tomatoes begin to brown and are very tender, about 35 minutes.

Meanwhile, toss cubed ciabatta with 1 tablespoon of olive oil. Season with salt and pepper then place on a baking sheet and bake until golden brown, about 10 minutes.

In a medium saucepan, heat the remaining tablespoon of olive oil over medium heat. Add the onion and sweat for 3 minutes. Add the white wine and reduce by half. Add all of the other ingredients, including the roasted tomato mixture and the toasted bread. Bring to near boiling, then reduce and simmer for 40 minutes. Blend until nearly smooth. Season to taste with salt and pepper.

GARLICKY CRUNCH: Garlic crumbs are a great way to use day-old bread. All you have to do is finely grind the bread into crumbs using a food processor. Then, in small batches, sauté the bread crumbs with garlic oil and butter until golden brown. Season with salt and pepper.

Stephanie Izard became the first woman to win Bravo's Emmy-nominated *Top Chef* in 2008 and is the chef-owner of Girl & the Goat, nominated for the 2011 James Beard Award for Best New Restaurant. She was also named one of *Food & Wine* magazine's Best New Chefs in 2011 and, along with Chicago-based food writer Heather Shouse, penned her debut cookbook *Girl in the Kitchen: How a Top Chef Cooks, Thinks, Shops, Eats & Drinks* (Chronicle Books, Fall 2011).

# SHRIMP AND ROASTED RED PEPPER CREAM SOUP

*from*

## CORINNE M. SACHS

Corinne came up with this elegant soup after dining with her daughters at Chicago's sorely missed Pepper Lounge years ago. She enjoyed it so much she went home and came up with this rendition, which has become a family holiday tradition. Her daughter Sheila prepared it for Soup & Bread using a more complicated fish stock that added depth to its flavor. It was worth the effort, but cooks be warned: her kitchen smelled like fish for days!

### INGREDIENTS        SERVES 12

- **2** red bell peppers, roasted and diced
- **2** pounds shrimp; cooked, shelled, and diced
- **1** tablespoon olive oil
- **1** cup onion, diced
- **1** cup celery, diced
- **6** cloves of garlic, minced
- **6** cups fish stock (see page 193)
- **½** cup parsley, chopped
- **6** tablespoons butter
- **6** tablespoons flour
- **2** cups sour cream (light)
- **1** cup heavy cream
- **2** sprigs of thyme
  salt and pepper to taste

### PREPARATION

Roast the red peppers over an open flame until blackened on all sides. Place in a paper bag for several minutes to allow steam to blister them.

Sauté the onions, celery, and garlic in olive oil until soft. Peel the skin off the cooled red peppers, and dice. Add them to the other vegetables, and continue cooking on medium heat. Add fish stock. Stir in parsley. Set aside on low heat.

Melt the butter in deep pan and add the flour a little at a time. Stir constantly over medium heat until mixture bubbles, thickens, and just begins to brown. Add the stock mixture slowly to the roux, stirring continuously. When all the stock and vegetables have been mixed into the roux, whisk in the cream and sour cream.

Tie thyme sprigs together with string and immerse in soup. Add cooked shrimp and simmer to blend flavors. Salt and pepper to taste. Remove thyme before serving.

Corinne M. Sachs is an avid swimmer, is fond of physical therapy, and still loves to create soup.

# FISH SOUP

*from*

## ROGER SIMON

Some of the donors to the Kickstarter fundraising effort for the first, self-published Soup & Bread Cookbook had their generosity rewarded with the dubious prize of having a soup prepared in their name and to their specs during Soup & Bread 2010. Roger provided this quick and easy recipe for fish soup. We used tilapia and added a quart of vegetable stock to stretch it out a bit, which resulted in a light, clean broth with a strong acidic backbone that really allows the fish to pop. The clams in their shells were also a big hit with the kids, who ran around performing clam puppet plays when the soup was all gone.

**INGREDIENTS**  SERVES 6–8

- **1** medium white onion
- **1** garlic clove
- **¼** cup olive oil
- **1** 8-ounce can chopped tomatoes
- **1** pound cubed, firm, strongly flavored fish (delicate fish like sole will disintegrate during cooking)
- **1½** cup dry white wine
- **8** ounces clam juice
- **½** pound frozen shrimp
- **½** pound cherry stone clams
- **½** pound bay scallops
- **4** cups vegetable stock (if desired)
- salt and pepper
- thyme
- Tabasco

# The Measure of a Chef

The first thing you learn in culinary school—after how to slice an onion and where to find the salt—is how to make stock. Enshrined by Escoffier as the foundation of classical French cooking, stock is the first step toward a multitude of sauces and braising liquids. But if you follow stock to its apotheosis, you'll arrive at consommé.

Soup at its most refined, consommé is the standard used to take the measure of a chef. A perfect consommé is crystal clear—so clear, writes Michael Ruhlman in *The Making of a Chef*, his first-person account of a year at the Culinary Institute of America, that "you should be able to read the date off a dime at the bottom of a gallon."

It starts out as a humble mix of bones and water, some carrots, a little onion. It's topped with an absolutely disgusting concoction of egg white and minced meat—the magical "raft" that draws impurities out of the liquid and into its gooey web. All the protein-rich stuff is an extravagance: it'll get tossed in the end. But after this rich mess is simmered, clarified, strained, and skimmed, what's left behind will sparkle, a flare signaling the diner that the meal to follow will be an expert affair.

## PREPARATION

In a large soup pot, sauté onion and garlic in olive oil until translucent. Add fish and simmer a few minutes. Add wine, clam juice, shrimp, clams, and scallops.

Simmer till shrimp turn red, clams open, and fish cubes are tender.

Even better the next day.

Roger Simon is professor of medicine and neurobiology at Morehouse School of Medicine, Atlanta, and author of *Clinical Neurology*, 8th edition coming soon.

# SCOTCH BROTH
*from*
## ROB AND ALLIE LEVITT

The husband and wife team of Rob and Allie, both vocal advocates for sustainably farmed meat and whole-animal cooking, made their culinary reputations as chef and pastry chef at Chicago's celebrated Mado restaurant, but left that gig in 2010 to open a butcher shop—which allows them to talk meat all day long. The secret to this potent broth is patience, as you simmer and reduce, and simmer and reduce over and over again. You'll be rewarded with something phenomenally concentrated, with a depth of flavor I had never before tasted. The shot of Scotch doesn't hurt either.

**INGREDIENTS**                    SERVES 16

**2** pounds lamb bones and water
**OR**
**24** cups lamb stock (see page 197)

**1** tablespoon fat, your choice (beef or pork fat, butter, and olive oil all work)
**1** onion, minced
**3** cloves garlic, minced
**1** sprig rosemary, leaves removed and chopped
**1** bunch baby turnips, cut into bite-size chunks
**4** carrots cut into bite-size chunks
**5** small potatoes, halved or cut into bite-size chunks
**1** small head green cabbage, finely shredded
**3** ribs celery, finely sliced
**1** shot good quality Scotch
salt and pepper

## PREPARATION

Arrange bones on a baking sheet or pan and roast at 350°F until brown. Remove from oven and cover bones with water in a large stockpot. Bring water to boil, then lower heat to simmer, skimming occasionally, for 6 hours. Strain to clarify and set aside.

In a heavy-bottomed pot, cook the onion, garlic and rosemary over medium heat until very soft, but not browned, in a tablespoon of the available fat of your choosing (though we don't recommend lamb fat). Add a pint of the lamb stock, and let simmer away until there is nothing left but a sticky brown goo on the bottom of the pan. Just as you fear it burning, add another pint and reduce again as directed above. (If you've got a lot of time, and a lot of stock, you can repeat the process as many cycles as you like.) Then add the remaining stock, save one quart, and simmer gently.

While that's simmering, place the carrots in a separate small pot and cover with as much of the reserved lamb stock as needed. Add a good pinch of salt and bring that to a gentle simmer. When carrots are tender and delicious, remove them to a plate to cool. (Note: the reserved carrots will be difficult to resist. If you sneak one here and there, before you know it, they'll all be gone. Carrots cooked in meat broth are delicious. You've been warned.)

Add the turnips to the broth and top off with reserved stock if needed. Proceed as above, remove to a plate to cool, and heed the same warning.

Cook the potatoes the same way as above. When the potatoes are done, remove those to a plate and add the juice they've been cooking in, and any remaining lamb stock, to the pot of simmering broth. All of this can be done a day in advance, if you like, and then finished just before dinner.

After the first round of aperitifs and light hors d'oeuvres, bring the broth up to a strong simmer and add the cooked vegetables. Then add the cabbage and celery (yes, raw) and taste. Add salt and pepper as needed. When satisfied, add the shot of Scotch. Scotch is, frankly, not a traditional ingredient in Scotch Broth but allows you a chance to sneak a nip of Scotch before returning to your dinner.

Serve in warmed soup bowls with thick slices of good country bread.

Rob and Allie Levitt are the owners of The Butcher & Larder, Chicago's first sustainable, whole-animal butcher shop.

# CHAMPAGNE AND LAMB
# FRENCH ONION SOUP

*from*

## MICHAEL NAGRANT

Michael's a prolific Chicago-based food writer whose credits include everything from *New City*, a free weekly paper, to the deluxe 2008 Alinea cookbook, for which he meticulously deconstructed the avant-garde restaurant's famed "Black Truffle Explosion." For Soup & Bread he served this intoxicating interpretation of a classic French onion soup along with a side of ethereal Parmesan-cheddar gougères. See page 182 for that recipe.

**INGREDIENTS**                    SERVES 12

- 1½  pounds yellow onions
- 8  tablespoons unsalted butter
      kosher salt
- ¾  teaspoons all-purpose flour
- 1  cup Champagne (dry brut style)
- 8  cups beef stock (Swanson is fine, homemade is better)
- 8  cups chicken stock (Swanson is fine, homemade is better)
- 4  medium stalks of fresh thyme
- 1  bay leaf
- 6  peppercorns
      (put thyme, bay leaves, and peppercorns in a cheesecloth and tie off to create a sachet)
- ½  lemon
- ½  pound lamb shoulder, cut in cubes
- 1½  teaspoons olive oil

## PREPARATION

Cut off tops and bottoms of the onions, then halve the onions lengthwise. Remove the peels and tough outer layers. Cut a V-shaped wedge in each one to remove the core.

Lay an onion half cut-side down on a cutting board with the root end towards you. Note that there are lines on the outside of the onion. Thinly slice onions into half-moons along the lines, i.e. with the grain. Cutting along the lines rather than against them will help the onions soften when cooked.

Melt butter in a large heavy stockpot over medium heat. Add the onions and 1 tablespoon salt, and reduce heat to low. Simmer for about 3 hours, stirring every 15 minutes. The onions will first wilt and release a lot of liquid. Continue to simmer and stir being sure to scrape the bottom and corners of the pot, until the onions are caramelized (i.e. dark golden brown) throughout. Remove from heat.

In an 8-quart or larger pot, heat olive oil over medium heat until shimmering; add lamb and caramelize until brown. Transfer about 1 cup of the caramelized onions (you may have more from the previous step, save for another application, pizza or sammies) to the pot. Sift in the flour and cook over medium-high heat, stirring for 2 to 3 minutes. Add the beef stock, chicken stock, and Champagne and simmer for about 1 hour.

Season to taste with salt, pepper, and a generous squeeze of lemon. You can also finish with a touch more Champagne or cognac when serving. Remove from heat.

Michael Nagrant never met an organ meat he didn't like. He hopes to meet many more.

# PORK DUMPLING GANG

*from*

## HUGH AMANO

This lovely soup is rather involved, but the results are worth the precisely machined effort. The recipe deftly combines Hugh's Japanese heritage and his love of pasta. "I made this soup during a time that I was working on making a broth that was my own, influenced by the great ramen shops of Japan," he says. "Plus, I love rolling and hand forming pasta, so I used a gyoza-type filling to make the tortellini. It is indeed an involved soup to make, but spending the day roasting bones and simmering pots while making tortellini is one of the more relaxing things in life."

**INGREDIENTS**

SERVES 6

ROASTED PORK BELLY

- **1–2** pounds pork belly, skin off
- **3** tablespoons kosher salt per pound of pork belly
- **3** tablespoons dark brown sugar per pound of pork belly
  fennel, cumin, Chinese 5-spice, coriander, or any other spices you might like

PICKLED MUSHROOMS

- reserved shiitake mushrooms from pork dashi, sliced thin
- **¼** cup pork dashi
- **½** cup cane vinegar
- **¼** cup soy sauce
- **1** tablespoon sambal (chile paste)
- **1** tablespoon freshly grated ginger

PORK DASHI: SEE PAGE 195

PORK AND GINGER TORTELLINI

DOUGH

- **1** cup all-purpose flour
- **2** large eggs
  pinch of salt

MAKES 24

FILLING

- **8** ounces pork shoulder or loin, cubed
- **2** ounces pork fat back, cubed
- **1** tablespoon freshly grated ginger
- **2** cloves garlic, finely minced
- **1** scallion, finely minced
- **2** teaspoon sambal
- **3** tablespoons cane vinegar
- **1** teaspoon sesame oil
- **1** teaspoon fish sauce
- **1** tablespoon soy sauce
- **1** tablespoon Thai basil, minced
- **1** tablespoon culantro (a cousin of cilantro, which may be substituted), finely minced
- **2** eggs (or 1 whole egg and at least 1 additional yolk)

## PREPARATION

PORK BELLY: Rub pork belly with salt, sugar, and your choice of spices. Put in a plastic bag and seal. Place in refrigerator and let cure overnight. If you can't do overnight, give it as much time as you can. Even an hour.

PICKLED MUSHROOMS: While the meat is curing, bring dashi, vinegar, soy sauce, sambal, and ginger to a boil. Pour over mushrooms and let cool. Cover and keep refrigerated. (These will keep for about a week.)

When pork belly is done curing, heat oven to 400°F. Remove pork from bag, discard any liquid, and place meat in roasting pan, fat side up. Roast for 60 minutes. Lower oven temp to 250°F. Roast an additional 60–90 minutes until outside is crisp and inside is tender. Remove from oven and let cool in a refrigerator. When cooled, slice into thin chunks.

TORTELLINI: Meanwhile, make the tortellini. Combine flour, eggs, and salt in a bowl and knead well until a smooth, cohesive consistency is reached. Let rest for 20 minutes. Roll to your pasta roller's thinnest setting and cut into 3-inch diameter circles. Keep covered so dough does not dry out.

Grind pork and fat, or finely mince. Add ginger, garlic, sambal, vinegar, sesame oil, fish sauce, soy sauce, Thai basil, culantro, and 1 egg. Combine well. Poach a small sample and taste for seasoning, making any necessary adjustments.

Brush half of a dough circle lightly with a little egg yolk. Place a small amount of filling, roughly ½ teaspoon, in the middle of circle. Fold bottom of circle up to create a half moon containing the filling. To create tortellini shape, place the flat edge of the half moon across your pinky so it forms a cross with your pinky. Wrap the dough around your pinky, overlapping the two ends and pinching them down to seal. Use egg to help stick the two ends to each other if necessary. Remove from finger and place on floured sheet pan.

Steam or simmer tortellini until filling is cooked all the way through. Assemble dish by placing 4 tortellini in the bottom of a soup bowl. Add a few slices of pork belly and a few pickled shiitake mushrooms, arranging in an attractive manner. Sprinkle a pinch each of culantro, Thai basil and scallions in bowl. Present to your guests. At the table, ladle hot pork dashi into each bowl.

Chef, writer and general food lover Hugh Amano lives in Chicago and wants people to return to cooking. His writing on food can be seen at foodonthedole. blogspot.com.

# PARMESAN-CHEDDAR-THYME GOUGÈRES
*from*
## MICHAEL NAGRANT

Mike first tried these elegant bites at Thomas Keller's French Laundry in 1994, when the restaurant (famous for its hospitality) plied his party with Champagne and hot, savory cream puffs—usually infused with Gruyère—at the bar as they waited for their table to open up. "Maybe it was the bubbly talkin'," says Mike, "but the pungent cheese perfume and the salty pastry was a heady combo that I never forgot. These are really easy to make, and I've been making them ever since according to this modified Thomas Keller recipe."

### INGREDIENTS                MAKES 24 PUFFS

- 1 cup water
- 7 tablespoons unsalted butter
- 1 tablespoon kosher salt, or more to taste
  pinch of sugar
- 1¼ cups all-purpose flour
- 4–5 large eggs
- ¾ cup grated aged cheddar
- ½ cup grated Parmigiano-Reggiano
- 1 teaspoon fresh thyme
  freshly ground pepper

## PREPARATION

Preheat the oven to 450°F. Line two baking sheets with silicone baking mats or parchment paper.

In a medium saucepan, combine the water, butter, salt, and sugar and bring to a boil. Add all the flour at once, reduce the heat to medium, and stir with a wooden spoon for 2 minutes, or until the mixture forms a ball and the excess moisture has evaporated (if the ball forms more quickly, continue to cook and stir for a full 2 minutes).

Transfer the mixture to the bowl of a mixer fitted with the paddle (spray paddle with nonstick spray) and beat for about 30 seconds at medium speed to cool slightly. Add 4 eggs and continue to mix until completely combined and the batter has a smooth, silky texture. Stop the machine and lift up the beater to check consistency. The batter should form a peak with a tip that falls over. If it is too stiff, beat in the white of the remaining egg. Check again and, if necessary, add the yolk.

Finally, mix in ¾ cup of the cheese mix, along with 1 teaspoon of fresh thyme, and adjust the seasoning with salt and white pepper.

Fill a pastry bag fitted with a ⅜-inch plain pastry tip with the gougère batter. If you don't have a pastry bag (because who does?) just use a largeish Ziploc and cut the tip off one corner. Pipe the batter into 1-tablespoon mounds on the baking sheets (use a butter knife to cut the batter from the bag), leaving about 2 inches between the gougères as the mixture will spread during baking.

Sprinkle the top of each gougère with about ½ teaspoon of the remaining grated cheese and bake for 7 to 8 minutes, or until they puff and hold their shape. Reduce the heat to 350°F and bake for an additional 18–22 minutes. When the gougères are done, they should be a light golden brown color. When you break one open, it should be hollow; the inside should be cooked but slightly moist.

Michael Nagrant never met an organ meat he didn't like. He hopes to meet many more.

# BOULE WITH ONION JAM
*from*
## DEVON BERGMAN

Devon's partner Celeste is a professional baker and pastry chef, but Devon only started experimenting with baking in 2010. This tricked-out boule was an immediate triumph. Try making extra onion jam and just spreading it on crackers or toast for a special treat.

## INGREDIENTS
MAKES 4 LOAVES

### BREAD

- **3** cups lukewarm water (no warmer than 100°F)
- **1½** tablespoons granulated yeast (1½ packets)
- **1½** tablespoons kosher or other coarse salt
- **6½** cups unsifted, unbleached, all-purpose flour, measured with scoop-and-sweep method
  parchment paper for baking
  baking stone
  broiler pan

### ONION JAM

- **3** tablespoons unsalted butter
- **2¼** red onions, thinly sliced
- **½** bottle dry red wine
- **2** tablespoons ruby port
- **1½** tablespoons sugar
  salt and pepper to taste

## PREPARATION

Warm water slightly: it should feel just a little warmer than body temperature. If cold water is used, double the rise time.

Combine yeast, salt, and water in a 5-quart mixing bowl or large plastic container and give it a quick stir.

Add the flour all at once to the yeast, salt, and water. Mix with a wooden spoon until the flour is well incorporated; it should appear uniform with no dry patches. (No kneading is necessary.) This mixing should only take a couple of minutes.

Cover the bowl or container with a loose-fitting lid or sheet of plastic wrap, and allow the dough to rise at room temperature until it begins to collapse or at least flatten on the top (no less than 2 hours).

While the dough is rising make the onion jam, as follows: Melt butter in a heavy saucepan over medium-low heat. Add the onions, stir to coat with butter. Cook covered, stirring occasionally, until the onions are wilted but not browned, 20–30 minutes. Add the red wine, increase the heat to medium-high, and simmer, uncovered, until there is little or no liquid left, 40–50 minutes.

Add the port and the sugar and simmer until all the liquid has cooked away. Season with salt and pepper to taste.

Forming the boule: Sprinkle the surface of the dough with flour and cut off a one-pound piece the size of a large grapefruit. Dust hands and work surface with more flour if necessary. Again—no kneading is necessary. (The remaining dough can be stored in the refrigerator for up to 14 days with an airtight lid.)

Before forming the dough into a ball, create a pocket in the lump of dough with the handle of a wooden spoon and fill the cavity with jam. Gently pinch the pocket closed and repeat in another part of the dough until there's a random distribution of jam-filled pockets tucked deep within the dough (as few or as many as desired).

Dust hands with more flour if needed. To create a "gluten cloak," gently stretch the surface of the dough around to the bottom on all four sides, rotating the ball a quarter-turn as you go. The bottom of the ball may look like a collection of bunched ends, but it will flatten out in the resting and baking process.

Place the formed loaf on a sheet of parchment on top of an upside-down sheet pan. Rest the dough between 40 and 60 minutes before baking.

Twenty minutes before baking, preheat the oven to 450°F. Place a baking stone in the oven on the center rack and an empty broiler tray on the lowest rack.

After the boule has rested, paint the loaf with water and slash the top with ¼-inch deep cuts approximately 2-inch apart.

When the oven is fully preheated, slide the loaf with the parchment onto the baking stone from the upside-down sheet pan. In the broiler tray on the low oven rack, place ice cubes from two trays to create steam during the baking process. The loaf should bake until the crust is nicely browned and firm to the touch, approximately 50 minutes.

Let cool completely before slicing.

Devon Bergman has an abiding appreciation for all things handmade, acoustic, and shared with friends.

# CHAPTER NINE

# Stock

Good stock is the foundation of every soup and can mean the difference between something serviceable and something sublime. And while Soup & Bread is no stranger to the convenience of something store-bought, homemade stock is hands-down the best—and so easy to make! Many Soup & Bread cooks have provided stock suggestions over the years; between them these 8 recipes should meet most of your stock needs. Feel free to play with seasonings as desired. All should keep a week or two in the fridge or a few months in the freezer—though if you're going to freeze it I'd suggest simmering to reduce the stock in the pot by half before you do. What remains will be nicely concentrated, and can be reconstituted later by adding water. Freeze in repurposed yogurt containers or ice trays for handy single-serving portions.

# SIMPLE VEGETABLE STOCK
*from*
## CHRISTOPHER SULLIVAN

Christopher used this delicate vegetarian stock as the base for his caldo verde (see page 69). Which just goes to show you—vegetables aren't just for vegetarians anymore. In fact, a vegetable stock can provide a nice, light foundation for soups starring sausage and other strong meats.

**INGREDIENTS**                    MAKES 16 CUPS (1 GALLON)
- **2** large onions, white or yellow, coarsely chopped
- **3** stalks of celery
- **2** large peeled carrots
- bay leaf
- **10** or so whole peppercorns
- **16** cups water
- thyme and/or parsley, fresh or dried

**PREPARATION**

Place all ingredients in large stockpot, cover with water, and bring to a boil. Reduce heat and simmer about 30 minutes. Turn off heat, add herbs of your choice, cover, and let steep off heat for another half an hour or so. Strain and you're ready to go.

Christopher Sullivan is the chef at Ikram, a restaurant and boutique in downtown Chicago. He previously worked at Blackbird for many years.

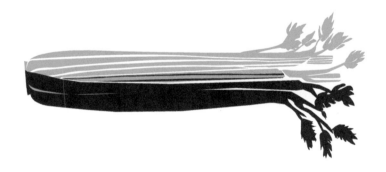

# ROASTED VEGETABLE STOCK
*from*
## CHUCK SUDO

Roasting vegetables for stock may seem like a fussy extra step—they're just going to get boiled to a pulp, and then tossed at the end, right? But roasting brings a richness and depth of flavor to your stock that's well worth the additional effort. You can use just about any vegetables you like, but steer clear of cruciferous veggies like cabbage and broccoli, as they'll get bitter and sulfurous when cooked too long.

**INGREDIENTS**                                    MAKES 20 CUPS (5 QUARTS)

- **1** large carrot, coarsely chopped
- **2–3** stalks of celery, coarsely chopped, including leafy ends
- **2** small zucchini, coarsely chopped
- **2** leeks, white and pale green parts only, including root end, sliced in half and cleaned under running cold water
- **1½** yellow onions, quartered (don't bother to peel the skin off)
- **2** red bell peppers, quartered and seeded
- **1** head of garlic
- **2–3** shallots, halved (don't bother to peel the skin off)
- **2** cups mushroom stems, any variety (caps reserved for another use)
  leaves from 4 sprigs fresh marjoram
  leaves from 4 sprigs fresh thyme
  extra-virgin olive oil
- **½** cup or so dry white wine or light beer (Chuck used Pabst Blue Ribbon)
- **12** cups water
- **½** cup canned crushed tomatoes
- **1** bay leaf
  kosher salt and freshly ground black pepper

## PREPARATION

Preheat your oven to 450°F. Place all vegetables except tomatoes on a rimmed baking sheet. Sprinkle with marjoram and thyme and then generously drizzle with olive oil. Using your hands, toss to get everything coated. Slide baking sheet into the oven and roast for 45 minutes, turning the vegetables with a spatula every 15 minutes. When the vegetables are finished roasting, transfer them to a deep pot.

Add water, tomatoes, and bay leaf. Cover and bring to a boil. Meanwhile, place the baking sheet over two burners and heat on medium high. Pour in the white wine and, using a whisk, deglaze the pan.

Add wine from pan to soup pot and return to a boil. Remove the lid, reduce the heat, and simmer for 45 minutes. Strain the stock using a colander set over a large bowl, pressing down on the vegetables to squeeze out as much liquid as possible. If you like, you can strain again and remove stray bits to make the stock very clear, but it's not necessary. You can also fish out the garlic head and squeeze the soft, sweet garlic inside into the broth for added flavor.

Chuck Sudo is the editor in chief of Chicagoist.com and "the last of the hard core troubadours."

# CHICKEN STOCK
*from*
## DANIELLE AND JASON BITNER

Danielle and Jason used this stock as the base for a chicken tortilla soup they whipped up for Soup & Bread in Brooklyn. We couldn't include their whole soup recipe, but their contribution is well represented by this ultraversatile, and easy, stock. They moved to Chicago later that year, and this stock reappeared at Soup & Bread in 2011, with a turkey leg thrown in for extra flavor, as part of a savory cauliflower chowder.

## INGREDIENTS          MAKES 20 CUPS (5 QUARTS)

- **4** pounds chicken carcasses, or legs, thighs, and bone-in breasts
- **1** large onion, quartered
- **4** carrots, peeled and cut in half
- **4** ribs celery, cut in half
- **1** leek, white part only, coarsely chopped
- **10** sprigs fresh thyme (a few teaspoons of dry works fine too)
- **10** sprigs fresh parsley
- **2** bay leaves
- **8-10** peppercorns
- **2** cloves garlic, peeled
- **2** gallons cold water

## PREPARATION

You need a big pot. Using a tall pot with a colander insert makes it easy to strain your broth.

Put chicken, veggies, and herbs in the pot, add water, and simmer uncovered over low heat for 4–6 hours. Don't let it come to a rolling boil or you'll get lots of yucky muck. Also, if you put chicken breasts in the stock, take them out after they've been simmering for 30–40 minutes. When they're cooked through remove all the meat and shred. Reserve meat for later but put the bones back in the pot and let them keep cooking.

Skim scum from the top of the pot every so often as it burbles away for several hours. When it's done, remove colander of vegetables and bones or strain through a sieve. Refrigerate stock overnight, then skim fat from surface before using.

Prompted by the birth of their daughter Hollis and the desire to be closer to family and friends, Danielle and Jason Bitner moved back to Chicago after living in NYC for several years. As the Betterment Society (bettermentsociety.com), they help produce and promote creative projects and businesses.

# FISH STOCK
*from*
## SHEILA SACHS

Sheila was so determined to do this delicate—if pungent—fish stock justice that she finagled the necessary carcasses from a fishmonger and carried them home on the bus. But if you don't feel like dragging dead fish all over town she also provides an effective shortcut below.

**INGREDIENTS**     MAKES 6 CUPS (1½ QUARTS)

- **2** pounds bones from white-fleshed, non-oily fish (such as flounder, sole, weakfish), rinsed under cold water
- **½** cup white wine
- **3** tablespoons shallots, chopped
- **1** carrot, sliced
- **1** stalk celery, sliced
- **3** springs parsley
- **½** teaspoon dried thyme
- **3** peppercorns
- **6** cups water

**PREPARATION**

In a medium stockpot, combine all ingredients. Bring to a gentle boil, skimming any foam that forms on surface. Reduce heat and simmer 30–45 minutes. Strain and refrigerate (or freeze) till ready to use.

**QUICK FISH STOCK**     MAKES 6 CUPS (1½ QUARTS)

- **3** cups water
- **3** cups shrimp broth
- **3** fish bouillon cubes

**PREPARATION**

Combine in a pot over low heat, stir until bouillon is dissolved, and you're done.

Sheila Sachs designed this book.

# DASHI

*from*

## MIKE SULA

Dashi is a basic stock used ubiquitously in Japanese cooking. It gets much of its flavor from kombu, a dried kelp that provides the salty, meaty backbone, and katsuobushi, which are dried, fermented, and smoked bonito tuna flakes. Keep it pure, as Mike did, or complicate things with pork and chicken, as Hugh does in the recipe that follows.

**INGREDIENTS**                    MAKES 10 CUPS (2½ QUARTS)

  **3**  strips kombu (dried kelp), washed
  **3**  packed cups shaved katsuobushi (dried bonito flakes)
 **10**  cups water

**PREPARATION**

Soak the kombu in the water until it is soft, then bring to a boil over medium heat, skimming the foam. Remove the kombu and add the bonito. Simmer on low for a few minutes while skimming. Take off heat and steep for 15 minutes. Strain.

Mike Sula is a food writer for the *Chicago Reader*.

# PORK DASHI

*from*

## HUGH AMANO

### INGREDIENTS

MAKES 8 CUPS (2 QUARTS)

- **3** pounds pork neck bones
- **10** cups cold water
- **1** large piece kombu
- **1** pound chicken backs or bones
- **1** ounce dried shiitake mushrooms
- **1** onion, diced
- **1** carrot, peeled and diced
- **3** scallions, sliced
- **¼** cup cane vinegar, or to taste
- **¼** cup soy sauce, or to taste
- **2** tablespoons fish sauce, or to taste
  juice of ½ lime

### PREPARATION

Heat oven to 400°F. Put pork neck bones on sheet pan and roast in oven for 45–60 minutes, flipping once. While bones are roasting, put kombu in large pot and cover with water. Bring to a boil, then remove from heat. Let steep for 10 minutes. Remove kombu.

Put chicken bones into the kombu water over medium heat. When the pork bones are done roasting, pour off any melted fat. Add roasted bones to the water. Put roasting pan over a high flame and pour a cup or so of water into the pan to deglaze it. Scrape the pan with a spoon or spatula to remove flavorful bits stuck to the bottom. Pour all of this goodness into the stockpot with the bones, adding water to submerge them.

Bring stock just to a simmer, and allow to simmer slowly (a bubble or two every couple of seconds) for about 6 hours, occasionally skimming any scum that forms on top. Replenish water every hour or so as necessary to bring it back to original level.

After about 5 hours, add mushrooms, onion, carrots, and scallions. Simmer for final hour. When the stock is done, remove from heat and let rest for 30 minutes or so. After resting, strain it through the finest strainer available. Reserve mushrooms to make pickled shiitake mushrooms (see page 180) and discard everything else.

Let stock settle and skim fat, saving for another use. Add cane vinegar, soy sauce, fish sauce, and lime juice to taste. This pork dashi should last about seven days.

Chef, writer, and general food lover Hugh Amano lives in Chicago and wants people to return to cooking. His writing on food can be seen at foodonthedole. blogspot.com.

# SMOKED PORK STOCK
*from*
## CARA TILLMAN

**INGREDIENTS**                    MAKES 16 CUPS (1 GALLON)

- ½  pound bone-in pork loin, chopped up in chunks
- 1  small smoked ham hock
- 1  teaspoon black peppercorns
- 1  bay leaf
- 3  sprigs fresh thyme and/or rosemary
- 16  cups water
- 3  tablespoons salt (or to taste)

**PREPARATION**

Place all in large stockpot. Bring to a boil, then reduce heat. Simmer approximately 3 hours, or until broth is rich and full. Strain to remove meat and herbs. Refrigerate overnight and skim fat from top before using.

Cara Tillman lives in Austin, Texas, where she's learning to be a teacher and working in a wine bar.

# BEEF OR LAMB STOCK
*from*
## MARTHA BAYNE

I don't make a lot of meat stock, but my local butcher (see page 176) gave me this pro tip: Try roasting half the bones before you brown the other half. It's an additional step, but you'll get more depth of flavor that way. Note that lamb has a much stronger flavor than beef—err on the side of less meat if you're working with lamb.

## INGREDIENTS
MAKES 8 CUPS (2 QUARTS)

- **2** tablespoons vegetable oil
- **1** large onion, roughly chopped
- **2** carrots, roughly chopped
- **2** stalks celery, roughly chopped
- **4** pounds beef or lamb shanks
- **2** pounds bones, with marrow
- **½** cup dry red wine
- **8** cups water
- **½** teaspoon salt
- **2** bay leaves

## PREPARATION

Remove meat from shanks and chop into large chunks. Set aside, and then roast about half the bones on a cookie sheet until browned, if desired.

Heat the oil until shimmering in a large, heavy-bottomed pot or Dutch oven. Add onion, carrots, and celery and sauté until soft. Transfer vegetables to a big bowl. Add meat and bones to pot in batches (don't crowd the pot) and brown for 5 minutes per batch, or until meat is cooked relatively evenly on all sides. Remove meat and bones to bowl full of veggies.

Add wine to pot and cook, scraping gook from bottom of pot and incorporating, until liquid has reduced to about 3 tablespoons. Return meat, bones, and vegetables to pot; cover and reduce heat to low. Sweat all for about 20 minutes, until the juices run from the meat. Turn heat up to high; add water, salt, and bay leaves and bring to a boil.

Once boiling, reduce heat to low, cover pot, and simmer at least 2 hours, longer if you like. Skim foam from surface occasionally.

When done, strain and discard meat, bones, and vegetables. Let cool and skim fat before using.

Martha Bayne wrote this book.

## DIY SOUP & BREAD

Want to host your own Soup & Bread? Great idea! Here's what you'll need to get started:

A VENUE: In Chicago, Soup & Bread's home base is a bar, and we've found bars, taverns, and clubs to be a good bet coast to coast, as Soup & Bread is an effective way to drive traffic their way during the early evening hours when business is otherwise slow. Plus, what goes better with soup and bread than beer? Find a civic-minded publican and it's a win-win situation for all. Other possibilities might be an art gallery, an events hall, a local church or school, or even a private home.

A CAUSE: Conceptually, Soup & Bread is a natural fundraiser for hunger-relief initiatives. But why stop there? In Seattle, a group of enterprising women held a private event to raise money for an agency providing transitional housing for the homeless. You could use it to fundraise for a new school playground or a community garden. Whatever your mission, identify folks working in the field and partner with them get the word out to their supporters. Invite them to staff an info table during Soup & Bread, or just offer to distribute leaflets on their behalf.

SOUP: When it comes to soup it's best to cast a wide net. If you tap a half-dozen or so restaurants, caterers, friends, and local notables to contribute, you'll easily create a broad base of support for your efforts. In Chicago we suggest that cooks make at least 2 gallons of soup, which is about the most the average person can whip up in the average home kitchen. But professionals often have the capacity to bring more, so don't stop 'em if they want to bring a 10-gallon vat of chili. Also, depending on the inclinations of your community, it's usually a good idea to explicitly solicit at least a few vegetarian soups. Invite the cooks to stick around to serve their soup and answer questions at the event. If they can't that's cool; just designate a server to cover their pot.

BREAD: Bread has such a short shelf life in the market that you'd be surprised how easy it is to find a willing donor. In Chicago, both La Farine Bakery and the culinary program at the Illinois Institute of Art contribute the bread for our event. Some bakeries will only donate to a licensed 501 C-3 non-profit, but others aren't so fussy—so just start asking around! You will probably have to go pick it up yourself, so a car is helpful.

PUBLICITY: Get the word out to the local media with a clear, comprehensive press release at least two weeks before your event. Be sure to highlight any newsworthy angles such as a hot-button issue or a celebrity chef—and don't forget to include your contact info. And, of course, work your social networks through Facebook and Twitter.

**TABLES AND CHAIRS:** Unless you're using a space with its own tables and chairs, you'll need to round these up as well, which can prove a bit of a logistical challenge. Figure out your capacity and hit up friends for their card tables and folding chairs. Or, go the easy route and rent them from a party supply company.

**GEAR:** Unless all your cooks are pros with their own soup warmers, you should collect as many slow cookers as you have chefs. These can be found cheaply at thrift stores, or borrowed from friends with the promise that you'll scrub them clean and return them pronto. Or, if you want to invest for the long term, a basic 7-quart Crock-Pot can often be found new for under $20. It's nice to provide ladles (though you can also ask cooks to bring their own) and thermometers to make sure the soup is piping hot. And of course you'll need bowls and spoons. In Chicago we use compostable disposables, but if your venue has a dishwasher you might want to consider going all out. Real soup spoons and pretty ceramic bowls can really class things up.

**AMBIENCE:** Speaking of class, nothing makes a divey little bar look cozier than some vintage flowered tablecloths and candles. We also have a bunch of breadbaskets that we line with tea towels. Figure out what little touches you can include to make your event special—in Seattle, for example, we came across a bunch of hurricane lanterns that, when lit, gave the room a warm, welcoming glow.

**PROGRAMMING:** Over the years people have asked if their band can play at Soup & Bread, or if we wanted to host a book reading, or a comedy set. We've always intentionally kept the event free of programming, on the grounds that we just want to provide a low-key space for people to talk, eat, and mingle. But we do often have DJs spinning background music, and our Seattle Soup & Bread was followed by a rock show, with the proceeds from that going into the donations pot as well. It's totally up to you.

**VOLUNTEERS:** Many hands make light work! As the organizer you're going to spend a surprising amount of time answering questions, so it's crucial to have at least a few dedicated helpers to bus tables, wash dishes, find more napkins, slice more bread, refill soup pots, etc. It can be quite helpful if at least one person in your crew has some food service experience.

Soup & Bread is an open-source concept, and can be as casual or as structured as you like. However your event comes together just remember to have fun! And let us know how it goes at soupandbread.net.

# INDEX

## VEGETARIAN-FRIENDLY SOUPS

## ACKNOWLEDGMENTS

SOUP & BREAD is a collective endeavor, and one that would not be possible without the goodwill—and good cooking—of everyone who's ever brought a pot of soup or a loaf of bread to the Hideout on a winter Wednesday. Many, many thanks to all of you. I am only sorry we could not include every single one of your culinary creations in our cookbook.

Similarly, this book would not have been possible without the help of many gifted and generous people. I am particularly grateful to Agate president Doug Seibold for his interest in our soup project and his patience and constancy. Thanks also to Agate's Diana Slickman for her practical advice on matters financial. Thank you to Susan Ginsberg, Laura Fox, Zoe Zolbrod, Amy Davis, Nance Klehm, and Mickle Maher for various forms of support in the initial writing of this book. And thank you to Anne Trubek and the whole crew at Belt for greenlighting this 2020 reprint.

Ten years ago my friend Karen Gerod, owner of the late lamented Swim Cafe, whose recipe for red pepper soup is on page 144, was a bottomless well of support and encouragement for all things Soup & Bread. In the years following her death in 2014, her sister Debra Gerod has generously supported our work in Karen's name. Thank you so much Debra, and thank you to everyone else who has donated money, or ever bought a T-shirt, an apron, or a hat.

The support and enthusiasm of everyone at the Hideout—especially owners Katie and Tim Tuten and Mike and Jim Hinchsliff and the most excellent ever-shifting Wednesday crew of Andrea Jablonski, Brandy Ricker, Jennifer McLaughlin, Ryan Hembrey, Mitch Cocanig, Jeremy Miller, Amy Gard, Gabriella Chevalier, Sullivan Davis, and others—has been critical to the success of Soup & Bread over the years. And thanks of course to our glorious volunteers, past and present, including Eiren Caffall, Amanda Zwald, Angelique Grandone, Jacqui Shine, Hope Williams, Sarah Bortt, Sarah Dandelles, and everyone who has ever pitched in to help—including all our DJs. We are so grateful to you all.

Many thanks are due my friend and former boss Alison True, for taking on the editing of this manuscript. I would be lost without her clear eye and sound counsel. And finally, Sheila Sachs's keen design sense and Paul Dolan's illustrations are as critical to the identity of this book as the words on the page. I cannot thank Sheila and Paul enough for their contributions to the whole.

MARTHA BAYNE is a senior editor with Belt Publishing, and a managing editor of *South Side Weekly*, a nonprofit newspaper dedicated to supporting culture and civic engagement on Chicago's South Side. She is the editor of several books, including *Rust Belt Chicago: An Anthology* (Belt, 2017) and *The Chicago Neighborhood Guidebook* (Belt, 2019), and the founder of the Soup & Bread community meal project. Her features and essays have appeared in *Belt Magazine*, the *Chicago Reader*, the *Chicago Reporter*, Puerto Rico's Center for Investigative Journalism, PRI/The World, *Eater*, the *Baffler*, and many other outlets.

PAUL DOLAN has been creating art for over 20 years. His work references are unlimited in style, with a technique that moves from digital to traditional methods and back again. His other illustrated books include *Everything Is Going To Be OK*, written by Ariel Stern, and *Goodnight Houston*, written by Jennifer and Kyle Solak. His work can be seen at dolandesign.com.

SHEILA SACHS is a graphic designer in Chicago. In addition to this and a handful of other books, she has designed several hundred LPs, CDs, and posters for a plethora of different record labels—although the bulk of her work has been for Thrill Jockey Records. She worked at the *Chicago Reader* for 22 years—more than half of those as the art director.

All royalties from sales of this book will be donated to the Greater Chicago Food Depository and to grassroots hunger-relief projects in Chicago.

*soupandbread.net*

"Soup & Bread has been a Chicago institution since it took over wintery Wednesday nights at The Hideout...Featuring contributions from Stephanie Izard, "Hot" Doug Sohn, and Paul Kahan, the book brings together a charming array of soup facts, recipes, and images that make readers just long for cold nights with a bowl of something starchy and pureed." — *THE A.V. CLUB*

"One of the most thought-provoking (and appetizing!) books I've picked up in a long time." — **TAMAR FLEISCHMAN,** *BALTIMORE EXAMINER*

"Martha Bayne's new book is a reflection on the cultural importance of soup as much as a cookbook...The book reflects the almost palpable enthusiasm for soup that can be felt at the [Soup & Bread] events." — **JULIA THIEL,** *CHICAGO READER*

"Beautifully written, generous and honest, the book looks at community building through lenses as various and diverse as the country has to offer. Bayne finds people of many kinds — immigrants, nuns, urban farmers, artists and activists — each using soup to bring people together and knit up what has become unraveled." — **EIREN CAFFALL,** *TIKKUN*

"There are a lot of interesting soup recipes in Soup & Bread, but to me the most motivating element of the book is the chapter introductions, which outline the various ways that people can use soup to 'build community one pot at a time." — **LINDA FALKENSTEIN,** *ISTHMUS*

"Soup is sometimes more than soup. It's sustenance, comfort, a lifesaver, and a social glue. Martha Bayne explores the social function of soup, weaving stories of soup swaps, soup kitchens, and soup feasts....The recipes are inspired and the dishes outstanding." — *TODAY'S DIET & NUTRITION*

"A significant document on the importance of food and community...A book of genuine people from all angles of life sharing food and recipes." — **HUGH AMANO,** *FOOD ON THE DOLE*

"Hot, tasty philanthropy." — *VILLAGE VOICE*